In His Grace

Grappling with Mesothelioma

The Randy Brady Clemmons Story

by Debbie Clemmons

In His Grace
Grappling with Mesothelioma
The Randy Brady Clemmons Story
By
Debbie Clemmons

Copyright © 2013

ISBN – 13: 978 1494249618

ISBN – 10: 1494249618

First Edition

Acknowledgements Page

I would like to thank my old flat mate, Jane Goldspring, who always believed, prayed, supported, called, and came to visit during my darkest of days. As a true saint, you never backed down or walked away. You told me I could do this. Thank you for your unwavering love.

I am truly grateful for our two boys, Brady and Garrett, who give me a reason to get out of bed every day. Every day I am so proud to be your mom. Both of you are growing up to be wonderful, godly men. Your dad in that "Great Cloud of Witnesses" is also very proud of you.

I'd like to thank Steven Kazan for sharing his knowledge of the laws concerning mesothelioma and the support and assistance to The Clemmons family has received over the great many years.

To Greg Baker, with Christian Affordable Editing Services, took two months going through my ramblings, my deepest appreciation.

And to Diane Farr who spent an afternoon with me giving me her "two cents" on publishing. Turns out it was worth more than a buck.

But mostly, I'd like to say thank you to each of you that has brought by a meal, gave one of us a ride, helped financially with our medical bills, sat with Randy, spent the night and who sent cards and prayed us through this tough time. Without you, there wouldn't be "this" story.

Dedication Page

For all the warriors on the war front that are helping us battle this nasty terminal cancer. Thank you for your tireless efforts in helping find a cure and making lives as comfortable as possible. May God always guide your way, direct your paths, and keep you safe. It was my honor to see you fight on the war front.

Contents

Introduction 5

Chapter 1: Who Are We? The Clemmons 9

Chapter 2: Something Is Not Right 22

Chapter 3: January 2007, Beginning Treatment 39

Chapter 4: February 2007 Treatments and Blessings 59

Chapter 5: Spring, Summer, and Fall of 2007—Easy Breezy 67

Chapter 6: Winter 2007—Getting a Port 78

Chapter 7: January 2008 - A New Year 88

Chapter 8: March 2008 Allergic to Altima 97

Chapter 9: May 2008 Holding His Own 104

Chapter 10: August and September 2008 Pain and Petco Park,
San Diego 113

Chapter 11: Pain Management 130

Chapter 12: October and November 2008 Radiation and
Disneyland 136

Chapter 13: December 2008 Christmas in Washington 145

Chapter 14: February 2009, New Pain Clinic and New Chemo 154

Chapter 15: March 2009, Appendicitis Again 162

Chapter 16: May and June 2008 Pain Pumps.............................. 170

Chapter 17: Goodbye to KFAX... 184

Chapter 18: August 2009 Time at Home.................................... 193

Chapter 19: Randy Brady Clemmons... 199

Chapter 20: The Memorial Service.. 221

Chapter 21: August 2013 Wrapping It up.................................. 223

Chapter 22: Randy Tributes.. 225

Chapter 23: How to Choose an Asbestos Attorney.................... 128

Chapter 24: Resources.. 260

Introduction

The reasons for this book are three fold. The first reason is to map out our experiences while fighting mesothelioma so other patients who are diagnosed with mesothelioma can get an idea of what to expect and obtain some ideas on how to fight. Hopefully, there will be some patients that can take the things that were successful and expand on them. The purpose of this book is not to give medical advice or to replace any medical advice. It is simply an account of our experiences. If you picked this book up for information on mesothelioma, it is my prayer that you are the person who finds the cure. I pray that you are the one that beats this and finally ends the suffering this cancer imparts. At the end of the book, I'll list our doctors and resources in case you want to reach out to them.

The second reason for this book is to be a testimony of God's love. When we were given a diagnosis of terminal cancer, we also found God wrapping us in His big quilt of love and huddling us in close to Him. I want readers to see how God inspired the community and the church to reached out and hold us up. It's an amazing story of love, hope and grace. It was a very painful and personal time for us, but we swung our doors open and let the world in. There was very little that we didn't share at the time—though this book will reveal a few painful occurrences that we did keep to ourselves. Now you'll know everything.

The third reason is to share Randy's personal battle with this tumultuous cancer. He was an amazing man of strength and character. He handled his illness with such grace, dignity and love. I want to open a window into his soul so that you may peek and see how he connected with God for strength and stamina, and I want you to understand how God reached back to Randy with His amazing grace.

This book is dedicated to all the saints who walked with us on the path of the "Valley of the Shadow of Death." It was such a heavy burden, and we are grateful you were there to help ease the load. We were truly blessed to have you by our side. I will be forever giving thanks and praises to God for each of you.

We give thanks to God always for all of you, making mention of you in our prayers. – 1 Thessalonians 1:2

This is a story of grace and miracles. We were broadsided by the diagnoses of mesothelioma. However, at every turn, we found daily miracles and grace. God placed His saints in our path at the right time.

I have learned the hard way what others have already learned. There is an enemy, a deceiver that destroys from within. It tries to rob you of your peace, joy and life. It is a wolf that hides in sheep's clothing, invading when you least expect it. That enemy is called cancer. I believe that it comes as close to being Satan as Satan himself is. It is a disease that needs to be rebuked, to be overtaken, to be jailed, and then to have the key thrown away. We are at war with an enemy that is so small that it slips in undetected at a cellular level. This enemy is hidden and can't be seen until it rears its ugly head.

But God is still on His throne! He brings His peace in the midst of the raging storm. He is our joy in the small day-to-day miracles. He answered prayers. He promises to stick closer than a brother. He also promises to never leave us. He is the hope when doctors have none to offer. He sends in His cavalry when the going gets tough, and when He does, He sends His best. He offers abundant life, support, and encouragement through the darkest of days. On rainy days, if you look up, you'll see His rainbow in the grey clouds. He picks us up after cancer treatments and places us on solid ground, giving us rest. He is our refuge in times of stress and radiation treatments. He is the lifter of our heads and hearts after we receive negative news about the scans. He goes before us and prepares places in hospitals, clinics and even up with Him in eternal glory. He is our glory. Through all of life's trials, we continue to praise Him, because of the great things He has done.

As you read on, you will see God's handy work woven in the threads of our day to day battle with our cancer called, mesothelioma. This is our story.

There is a friend who sticks closer than a brother. – *Proverbs 18:24*

"Come to me all who are weary and heavy-laden, and I will give you rest. Take my yoke upon you and learn from Me, for I am gentle and humble in heart; and you shall find rest for your souls. For my yoke is easy and My load is light." – Matthew 11:28, 29-30.

"Let not your heart be troubled; believe in God, believe also in Me. In My Father's house are many dwelling places; if it were not so, I would have told you; for I go to prepare a place for you. And If I go to prepare a place for you, I will come again, and receive you to Myself; that where I am, there you may be also." – John 14:1, 2-3

Chapter 1: Who Are We? The Clemmons

Photo taken near Seattle at a relative's wedding, August 2006.

We, the Clemmons, live in Pinole, California, just across the beautiful bay of San Francisco. We are a family of four, Randy, Debbie, Brady and Garrett. Randy, who had just turned 51 at the time of his diagnosis, was a radio personality at KFAX radio in Fremont, forty-five miles south of Pinole, which was a bit of a commute. He was the morning drive time host. He rose from bed dark and early to greet commuters at 5 a.m. He brought a bit of light and joy to those preparing for a dreary work day.

Randy had the most beautiful bass voice, and he loved to speak, sing, and share his love for the Lord. He had a quick wit, loved to share a joke, and had a good, kind heart. He was an A's and Giants baseball fan and would schedule family vacation days around the "fellowship" days at either ball park. His favorite part of KFAX was his Sunday music show called, *"Spirit of Praise."* He would showcase some of the top Christian music artists and praise and worship songs. He was in his element on the music show, and it was there he thrived.

For years he worked out with weights. He was very strong and healthy. We would tag team our workouts. He would work out on the way home from work, come home, eat dinner and then I'd go back out to the gym. When I arrived, there would still be guys there from Randy's workout, drooling as they speak about how he bench pressed 325 lbs, 8 times! Then they would go on to talk about how big his biceps were and, "Oh man his pects". It was odd, to hear other men bragging on my husband, like a girl with a school crush. Randy dreamed of being in body building contests, but didn't have the confidence. That's why when he first presented symptoms, I didn't worry. I thought whatever this was he would be fine.

I loved the way he said, "Good morning," to me and the way he loved me so totally and completely. We rarely had fights or disagreements between us. Even when my thyroid went out and I gained weight, he never complained about it. Oh, things weren't perfect of course. We did have difficulties from outside influences, which did cause a great deal of strife in our house. In hindsight, some boundaries would have been helpful, but that is material for another book or a Dr. Phil show. We were an average married couple. We were married for twenty-four years and we both were committed to our Lord. Our marriage worked because of our faith.

Here is a photo of Johney & Juanita Clemmons. Unlike me, Randy grew up in a Christian home in San Pablo, CA. His Father, Johney, had an asbestos lung disease and died from it when Randy was 26. His mother, Juanita, raised him and his three sisters on Rollingwood Drive. They all were members and fellowshipped at First Baptist Church in Richmond. Randy, his dad, and sister loved to ride horses, and for years, they kept some horses at Hobb's Stables on San Pablo Dam Road. He attended Rancho Elementary, Helms Jr. High and De Anza High Schools in El Sobrante. Randy also was a part of a Gospel group called, "The Forever Family," along with his brother-in-law, and they sang on tours throughout the Western United States. He sang with *Reprise* from First Baptist and went

on youth choir tours. He taught Sunday School classes to Junior High and High School boys at Richmond First Baptist. Later, he sang with a quartet group called, "4 Given," and was featured in many solos. He attended the Columbia School of Broadcasting in Santa Rosa, CA. He really did have an amazing deep, bass voice.

Randy was also very much involved with NorthShore Community Church. Actually, the whole family was involved too. Randy, along with Brady, our son, helped in the children's ministries on Sunday mornings with Ron Kennedy. I was involved with women's ministries and helped out with the Jr. High and High School Sunday School Class with Beau Coffron.

Randy was also a big part of a men's soft ball team. For over ten years, he managed a group from First Baptist of Richmond. He led a team of guys to victory in countless tournaments and leagues. Many times they would return and throw big victory parties, but I believe the thing he embraced more than anything was the lifelong bonds made with this "band of brothers." Randy loved these men! They were his brothers, not only in Christ, but he felt deeply for them here on earth. There were lots of laughs and good times.

Top Row: Mike Lopez, Tom Emmons, Randy Clemmons, Scott Christensen, Donny Maestas, Brian Christopher, Ron Lawson
Front Row: Mark Leopold, Craig James, Jack Cranefield, Dave Rodden, Sara Lawson (Wright), Kirk Kirtchgater & Buster Donohue in front

Our oldest son, Brady, was 15 in his sophomore year at John Swett High School in Crockett when Randy was first told he had terminal cancer. Brady is a martial artist and has been taking karate since kindergarten at Ylagan Martial Arts in Pinole. He was dedicated to nearly the exclusion of other sports. A friendly fellow, Brady never met a stranger who didn't become a friend within five minutes. Brady also has a talent, a real gift in art. He can draw and paint—a talent I suspect he got from his Uncle Rick. He is currently working on a graphics art degree while working part time at the church and for an electronic repair shop. Since Randy's passing, Brady went on to get his black belt with Dumlao Martial Arts. A mom couldn't be prouder. Brady has had to overcome some major obstacles to get where he is today.

Garrett, who was ten at the time of Randy's diagnosis, was in the sixth grade and the biggest Sponge Bob fan ever. One look at his closet would convince you of his Sponge Bob passion. In addition to that, he loved playing basketball and soccer—and going out onto the field to toss a softball around with dad. Garrett, like his dad, was a jokester, always cracking up, trying to find jokes, telling jokes, and being sneaky.

He was only thirteen when Randy died, much too young to say goodbye. His dad was a big part of his heart and I know that it's hard on him to wake up every day without his dad around to harass him. He is very active in the youth group at Pinole Community Church. Recently, we found out that he too has Uncle Rick's talent for art. Not sure where Garrett will go with it, if anywhere. Garrett is still in High School at Pinole at the time of this writing. He has lots of time to decide what he wants to do. Maybe he'll end up with a deep bass voice and we will hear him on the radio. Who knows? He can do anything that God leads him to do.

Then there is me, the wife: "My trouble and strife" as Randy used to joke with me. We heard that rhyme on a trip to Australia. He would fondly say, "The Mrs…My Cheese and Kisses." Randy would always answer the phone, "Debbie's happy husband speaking." As I told you—he was a jokester. And he was also a happy man. Before Randy died, he had "Debbie's Happy Husband" engraved on the back of a heart locket for me and gave it to me for our last Valentine's Day. He always wanted me to remember how happy he was with me…it is so hard to write this with tears streaming down my face.

I came down to California in 1977 when I was seventeen. I was a brand new Christian from Bremerton, Washington. I had just been baptized one month earlier at Silverdale Baptist Church—now known as Grace Point. That is when I met Randy, but we didn't date until I was 21. I came to First Baptist Church and got involved with the youth group when I was a junior in High School. I got a job at Nation's Giant Hamburgers, and Randy's dad would show up and order pie from me. He would then try and talk Randy into dating me.

One day Johney Clemmons and Evans Lovelace offered Randy fifty bucks to take me out. Randy replied, "I won't be bought!" On our wedding day, Evans came over with a sock full of fifty dollars in quarters, saying he felt robbed that he had to pay the whole thing. Johney passed away from asbestoses before Randy and I started dating. I so wish I could have gotten to known Randy's dad better. I know he would have been a fabulous father-in-law. I hope he knows that Randy did ask me out, and we did date, got married, and he has two fabulous, wonderful grandsons. Garrett looks a lot like him, dark and handsome, just a lot taller!

For over thirty years, Randy and I were both involved in youth ministries, choir, music, Bible studies, advisory boards, and where ever else we were called to be used. We were involved with so many people over the years that, when Randy did get sick, we had a great number people come and

15

help. My family was up in Washington and New York, so we were left alone to deal with getting to treatments, shopping, surgeries, and taking care of the boys. But truly, alone we were not! Our brothers and sisters in Christ were there—over two hundred of them. A few people who helped were listeners on KFAX who didn't even know us. My Bible study group was so supportive. They continually brought dinners over on chemo nights. Others would offer to help give rides, and the list goes on and on.

For the past twenty-five years, I had been working for billboard advertising companies and traveling around the country to meet with marketing companies and advertising agencies. I would put together advertising plans for companies, execute contracts, place ads up, and orchestrate advertising and marketing strategies. For the past ten years, I worked part time and took care of the home and boys. I was involved in karate with Brady and earned my black belt in my old age. It was a bit of juggling, but it all worked out just fine. Little did I know that the skills I learned in karate would come in handy when I was so tired and felt like giving up. I would have to force myself to keep moving forward, because martial artists don't quit. They don't give in, or lose focus, and they don't tap out. However, this gal didn't get her belt without a lot of prayer for wisdom, strength and stamina. I know where to tap into the highest power source.

When Randy went to work in broadcasting, his dream job, he took a significant pay cut and lost the health insurance for the whole family. He received health benefits from his new job, but to add the entire family to the policy meant we would have to pay out of pocket for the premiums. They were a bit steep, so I paid for a county plan that wasn't as expensive at the time. Now it is my biggest expense.

Randy's new job also meant that he added a 90 mile daily commute to get to the station and back. In no time at all, our savings were drained. For a while, I worked weekends, cleaning apartments since it was such a struggle to pay our bills. We hunted for ways to cut our budget. I would shop at the dollar store before going to the grocery store. We kept our heat down in the winter by using the pellet stove for heat. At one point, Randy's spending money was five dollars a week.

I remember good friends telling me that God would understand if we didn't tithe. However, we always tithed, no matter what came in or how big or small it was. I worked on commission, and sometimes, I did have a good month. Regardless, we gave on the gross amount. Everything we have belongs to God, even our very breath, and I knew He would work the rest out. We also continued to give, what we could, to Young Life and the local rescue mission. We had a roof over our heads and were able to buy food. There are many homeless people out there, and only by the grace of God did we avoid that end ourselves. This is true for everyone. None of us are exempt. Life happens.

Soon, a position opened up where I worked for someone to put up posters and clean the bus shelters on the weekends. Randy got the part time job, and it worked out super, helping so much with finances. He would take Brady along and they would have some father-son bonding time. Looking back now, I realize how priceless that time together for them was. When Randy received the diagnosis of terminal cancer, everything changed. Nothing else matters when someone is sick. You hit your knees, praying for God's guidance and strength—especially when the doctors are telling you there is no help, no cure, and no hope. When that happens, you really do literally get on your knees and pray. Where else do you go, but to God, the maker of Heaven and Earth?

I often say we were like a four legged chair, and now we are like a three legged stool. It's so hard not to have a husband, a father, a friend here in the house to talk about the important and the trivial matters of life. When it is time for Randy to walk in the door from work, it's like the air is stifled. I sit in anticipation of hearing the engine of his truck coming up the hill into the driveway, but it never comes. Sitting at the dinner table and looking at his empty place was so painful and hard. We rarely sit at the table as a family now. It's just too difficult. We had an arrangement where Randy would cook dinner on Tuesdays and Thursdays. Well, Taco Bell had a promotion going on Tuesdays, so Randy would pick up tacos on those days. The boys loved it. I still will pick up tacos on some Tuesdays, just because Randy did. On Thursdays, Randy would cook a can meal. He would open up cans. It was truly interesting and sometimes even good.

It's hard to find the "new norm" as others call it. Even now that it is has been four years, the hole is still so big and our hearts still ache. I tell the boys their dad is watching them "in that great cloud of witnesses" and to make him proud. Randy did leave them big shoes to fill. Our work here is not done yet. That is why God still has us here, to complete the work He has for us to do. So we continue on as a family of three, with Jesus leading the way.

The righteous cry out, and the Lord hears them;
he delivers them from all their troubles.
The Lord is close to the brokenhearted
and saves those who are crushed in spirit.
(Psalm 34:17-18)

One more thing I'd like to say here. While we were dating, Randy made his first DJ tape and gave it to me on Valentine's Day. It was called, "Love Songs for Debbie." We had been dating for over four years at the time—Randy doesn't make sudden moves. While working on a roof one summer, his dad nicknamed him "Lighting" once as a joke. The tape was full of wonderful love songs. I had it for a few months and then one day it just disappeared. I was afraid to say anything, thinking I'd find it one day.

Naturally, Randy had to ask me about that tape. We were walking to the car from a boat christening and I had had a sip or two of champagne. I told him not to worry about the tape. I would find it. He said, "What do you mean?"

"I'll find it one day," I replied.

"When?" he asked.

"I don't know. One day."

"But when?" he persisted.

I said, "One day when I move. I'll probably find it then."

"When you move? When would you move?"

19

I told him, "I'm not going to live in this apartment forever? We've been dating for over four years now. One day you are going to marry me, aren't you?"

He ran away from me, yelling, "You're drunk! You're drunk!"

I just rolled my eyes, shaking my head, and we drove home after he came back chuckling.

The next day, he came over to my apartment, which I had shared with a friend, Jane, for over six years. He gets down on one knee, grabs my hand, and tenderly says, "Yes."

I asked, "Yes?"

He said, "Yes, I accept."

"You accept what?"

"Your proposal for marriage."

"Oh, no," I said, "that doesn't count. I want moonlight, flowers, dinner. I want the works! You don't get off this easy!" Well, he wasn't taking no for an answer. I think he was afraid to ask me to marry him, and the tape was going to be his gateway.

After his passing, I was in the garage, going through a box of his old trophies and tapes, and guess what I found? Yes, you guessed it. My "Love Songs for Debbie" tape. That sneak took my tape all those years ago. But what I want to share with you is a line of two of the lyrics of one of the songs: "If anyone should ever write my life story. For, whatever reason, there might be. You'll be there between line of pain and glory, because you're the best thing that ever happened to me." It's like Randy somehow knew, all those years ago, that there would be pain, glory and a story. Here I am all these years later, writing his story. Or did God orchestrate the whole thing? One day we will know.

Chapter 2: Something Is Not Right

Actual Copies of Internet Updates

December 19, 2006

Randy is at Alta Bates Hospital in Berkeley. He came home and said his chest felt full. We went to the emergency room. His left lung is full of fluid—again. We just drained his lung on December 8th and 3.75 liters of fluid came out. We haven't gotten the test results from that yet. The pulmonologist will come in tomorrow to drain his lung again and hopefully look a bit closer for some answers.

When we had the CT scan done on the 13th, he had 2 liters of fluid on his lung then, but nobody told him. He even took a DVD of the scan to his doctor (pulmonologist) on Friday, called on Monday, and her office said, "Everything was fine." But we are guessing he now has the 3.5 liters back on his lung.

The CT scan didn't show any tumors. So we can take a deep breath...please keep us in your prayers, that we will find an answer. I'll let you know tomorrow what's new. Debbie…

December 20, 2006

I just spoke to Randy on the phone. He is still at Alta Bates. The doctor came in at 4:00 a.m. and drained 3.4 liters of fluid off the lung. The next step is to get a CT scan without fluid in the lung, so they are scheduling that right away.

I will also figure out how to get his heart checked out. All that fluid had squished his heart and moved it over. I'll let you know more when we get home. Thank you for all the prayer and support. Debbie…

<u>December 20, 2006 PM (five days before Christmas)</u>

Well, I wish I had good news, but I don't. Randy's doctor told us today that the fluid from his lungs has cancer cells. The cells are mesothelioma cells, a rare type of lung cancer caused by working with asbestos. The fluid they tested is from the fluid they took off his lung on Dec. 8th—the first time we came to the emergency room.

The doctors don't know the extensiveness of the cancer and will do surgery on Friday morning to determine what we are looking at. Once the surgery is done on Friday and they know what they are dealing with, he will be scheduled to go to UCSF and they will

23

remove his left lung. The doctor feels that we need to be aggressive, and because Randy is in great shape and just turned 51, they think he will do fine with just the right lung.

I know each of you love us and send us your best. I'll send another e-mail Friday afternoon and let you know how the surgery went. In the meantime, send up your prayers. I am picking up the boys right now, and taking them to the hospital. We will tell them what is going on. I am choosing to hang onto my faith. God is on His throne and He won't give us more than we can handle. We will probably be spending Christmas at Alta Bates. You can call. Thank you so much for your love and prayers. It means more to us than you know...Debbie...

December 21, 2006

Here is a photo of Randy now. He goes in for surgery at 8:00 a.m. tomorrow. If the cancer is localized, they will remove the lung tomorrow. The plan is to go in, scrape the lining, look for tumors, take biopsies, and maybe remove a lung. Because of the fluid, Randy has been functioning on one lung for about a month now, so they think he will tolerate one lung just fine. His color and spirits were both up today. I will be at the hospital for the next two days with him in ICU. I will call one of my aunts and they will email to everyone the status. Thank you for your prayers; we will gladly take every one. We send our Christmas blessings to you and your family. Here's to a Happy Healthy New Year! Debbie...

December 22, 11:00 PM

I just wanted to update you on the surgery today. Randy did very well, and is recovering just nicely. He was in surgery for 3½ hours. The doctors were planning to take the lung, but the cancer has spread to other organs. The surgeon decided that if he did take the lung, he would have to take the pericardium and lining of the diaphragm. By taking the lining of the diaphragm it would open a pathway for the cancer cells to get to the good right lung. This mesothelioma, as I am finding out, is a very sneaky cancer that attacks the lining of the organs and then it builds tumors.

So the surgeon removed the lining of the lung. This way fluid wouldn't continue to fill it up. He scraped as many cells away as he could and is recommending that Randy go on chemo and radiation. After six weeks, they will reassess the situation. If Randy needs to have the lung removed, it will be done at UCSF or Stanford.

The surgeon said that Randy was the healthiest patient he has had with this cancer and feels that the chemo and radiation might just save his left lung. He said the lung tissue is really still healthy, even though there is a tumor there. Randy will be at Alta Bates until Wednesday or Thursday. Thank you for your support and encouragement and prayers! Blessings, Debbie…

<u>December 24, 2006</u>

Thank you so much for your emails, calls, milk, and especially all your prayers. People have asked to be added to the "update" list.

We met the oncologist yesterday, and we will start a hard dose of chemo & radiation after the New Year. Randy has to recover from the surgery. The incision goes from his back, almost where his spine is, all the way around to the front. His anesthesiologist, Dr. Sloan, said Randy was doing remarkable well.

Last night, Randy had an infection, so the doctors have started him on antibiotics. Randy was in a lot of pain, but Dr. Sloan was on duty and was able to increase the medication in the epidural.

It is our prayer that chemo/radiation treatments will be the end of this. Randy doesn't want to think about the big picture, just one day at a time. He is a big strong man and very healthy. Our church is committing people to pray daily for him this morning. We believe in prayer. Blessings to all of you, Debbie...

<u>December 27, 2006</u>

We were able to bring Randy home today. He is in some pain and sleeps on and off. He is moving around a bit as well. Our next step is to heal from this surgery and then see an oncologist. We will hopefully make an appointment tomorrow. Randy will go to the Alta Bates Cancer Treatment Center in Berkeley, which used to be Herrick Hospital, where Randy was born. Keep us in prayer. We see God's hand on us. Blessings, Debbie...

<u>December 31, 2006</u>

Thank you for all your prayers and support. I'd thought I'd update you on where we are on the last day of 2006. Randy has been home since Wednesday, recovering from surgery. It's been a painful process. However, he has been able to get outside and walk the courts a few times. He went to church this morning and was prayed for.

We have an appointment with Dr. David A. Pfister at the Alta Bates Comprehensive Cancer Center on Wednesday, January 3rd, at 3:00. He will determine at that time if Randy is strong enough and has recovered from surgery enough to start the chemo.

The oncologist in the hospital recommended two types of chemo: Carboplatin and Alitma for this type of cancer. These chemo treatments were done at John Hopkins during their clinical trials while she was studying there. It shouldn't make him nausea, but will make him very tired.

Keep us in prayer. I'll give you another update after the oncology appointment. Blessings, for a Happy New Year, Debbie…

One piece of advice I'll give you right now if you find yourself in a situation similar to mine. It's one I wish I knew about. *Start keeping receipts and keeping track of time spent taking care of loved ones. Write down the time spent at pharmacies and keep logs of time on the phone spent with hospitals, clinics, and caregivers.* There will come a time when someone—a lawyer perhaps—will want copies of receipts and want to know how much time was spent. Without these receipts and logbooks, you won't remember. To go back and remember all these things will be too difficult and overwhelming. So to have them as you go along will be blessing to you later.

You might want to keep a log of every bottle of 7-Up, ginger ale, antacid you buy or how much time you spent cleaning up after someone who is sick. Workman compensation will reimburse you for your care giving time—if you have records of it. Maybe keep a journal. Keep an envelope to keep your receipts in.

Another note on pain medication: If the insurance companies won't authorize pain meds, they may not be working with certain manufacturers. So you may want to try changing brands or doses. Sometimes, ten 50 mg tablets won't be authorized by their systems, but twenty 25 mg tablets will. So ask your doctor to write out the prescription a few different ways, especially if you are having problems. Some of the authorization centers are located out of the country—honest— like the Philippines. If the problems are always getting enough pain meds, then going on hospice will get you the meds you need. However, not everybody is always ready to go on hospice.

Another tip: Bring something to keep you entertained and busy at the cancer center and hospital. Things often don't go as planned, and you are there hours longer than expected. So having a movie, book, or project handy will help ease the time and anxiety. In fact, I began to plan for something *not* to go right. A classic example is the lab closing down for a few hours so you have to wait for them to reopen to get the blood work done. Occasionally, we had to wait for blood from the blood bank or maybe a doctor is running late from a surgery. At any rate, be prepared.

Debbie's Thoughts

"Spirit of Praise" Radio show, March 7, 2004
Randy introduces the Katina's song,
"Draw Me Close."

"A lot of times when things happen to you, do you try and figure out why? Sometimes I try and figure out just what His plan was and

His intentions were when different things happen in my life. Isaiah 55:8-9 says, 'For my thoughts are not your thoughts, neither are your ways my ways, says the LORD. [9] For as the heavens are higher than the earth, so are my ways higher than your ways and my thoughts than your thoughts.' We can't figure Him out, we just draw closer as we worship Him. Randy Brady, 100.7, The Bridge."

It was early December of 2006, and Randy came in huffing and puffing from playing some basketball with our ten year old son. He usually didn't huff and puff like this, so I asked him, "What's wrong?"

"Just can't catch my breath," he replied.

He had gone to a checkup earlier in the year and everything had come back perfect! So I wasn't too concerned. However, he is fifty-one, so I told him he had to see his doctor the next day. Later, to make sure, I called him at work and asked him if he had made the appointment or if he needed me to make it. He did and went to see his doctor.

The EKG at the doctor's office was way off. So Randy's doctor ordered a blood test and x-ray. It was Wednesday, and Randy couldn't get in for the x-ray until Friday. But Friday afternoon, Randy came home and said, "Get someone to take care of the boys and take me to the emergency room." The x-ray had shown that his left lung was full of fluid. I really didn't think anything of it. Randy was strong and healthy. If he had fluid on his lung, they could drain it and he would be fine.

A pulmonologist was called in and she compared the x-rays to the ones Randy had gotten eight months earlier. The older x-rays were pristine, so maybe these latest ones only showed a fluke—a onetime irregularity. Later that night the doctor drained 3.75 liters of brown amber fluid from his lungs. It reminded me of beer. That is equivalent to nearly two, two liter soda bottles. The doctor then ordered a CT scan and we went home.

Randy had another CT scan about a week later, and it showed another two liters of fluid back on his lung. However, nobody from the doctor's office picked up the phone to let us know. Randy went to the pulmonologist's office several times trying to get a reading on the CT scan, and they just told him he was fine. However, we found out weeks later in the emergency room that that was not the case. Nobody had looked at the CT scan for weeks! Can you believe that?

I remember how hopping mad I was that day. I was ready to scream and there must have been steam blowing out of my ears. Why didn't anybody look at that CT scan and get Randy in sooner to get that fluid off his lung? By the time the doctors drained it, it was over three liters. I wanted to take two of those two liter bottles of soda into the pulmonologist's office and say, "Try breathing with this in your lungs...and, oh, have a Merry Christmas!" That was my anger talking. I didn't really do it. See? I do have a filter.

I don't understand why nobody checked the second CT scan results. In the previous two weeks before finding out, Randy had called the pulmonologist office three times and went in twice to try and review the results. The office manager just said, "You're fine." I called Randy's primary doctor and asked him to be point person from then on out. He would have never let Randy walk around with fluid on his lung. We chose not to work with that pulmonologist or her office again. I would not recommend her to anybody else either.

As I look back, this is one of the smallest blunders of Randy's health care. It really gets unbelievable. It is only by the grace of God that I'm not in jail for battery and assault. You'll know why after reading the rest of this book. I firmly believe that someone should have been incarcerated for the mismanagement of Randy's care. These are supposed to be trained professionals. Well, keep reading; you won't believe what happens either.

I often wondered if I should include the whole story in this book, but I came to the conclusion that the only way to tell the story was to be real and tell you everything. Hopefully, others patients coming behind us will be prepared to take action if a similar situation should occur. You really must have an advocate to fight for the patient's rights. So, if you haven't done so, I'm advising you to get a healthcare directive executed. Even with the healthcare directive, I had to battle with hospitals, pharmacies, and insurance companies to get information, medication, treatments, procedures, and get medical bills paid.

It is of the upmost importance to keep a copy of your healthcare directive and power of attorney with you at all times.

I had to fax Blue Cross the paperwork four times. They just couldn't seem to find it and would not communicate with me until I resent it to them. If the person you are speaking with doesn't have a copy of the healthcare directive in front of them, because it is in a file somewhere else, they will not speak with you.

While all this was going on, Randy was in the hospital waiting for the result of his tests. I was praying and hoping, and that's when the doctor came in and told us that Randy had cancer. I couldn't believe my ears. I didn't want to believe it. I *couldn't* believe it…but I had no choice.

Randy had cancer!

What a shock, particularly after her office told Randy he was fine. I kept thinking it was some glitch that could be worked out, but she said, "I'm sorry. It is terminal and there is no cure. I'll send in a thoracic surgeon to talk to you." Then she walked out. Wow. I was numb and spinning with disbelief. Maybe she was wrong…she had been wrong a few weeks earlier. I just started crying, thinking this can't be true. Randy was really calm about it, like he understood. In fact he did. His dad had died of asbestosis.

I also recall a moment that seemed pretty amazing. After the pulmonologist told us Randy had cancer and left our room, within minutes Ron and Kellie Kennedy came walking in. They just "happened" to be shopping nearby and wanted to see how Randy was doing. Ron and Kellie were the children's ministers whom Randy and our older son, Brady, helped on Sunday mornings. We knew them very well and they were great friends. When they walked in, I had been crying. We didn't even have a chance to call anybody yet with our devastating news, and here they were to pray with us and counsel us. Ron advised us to be straight with the boys. Children were very smart and would know if we were lying to them. I don't even remember how the boys got to the hospital. I believed I did go and pick them up, but I don't recall. I remember Randy and I took them to the cafeteria and gave them the news. It was so hard to absorb. However, we all had a good cry.

Garrett said, "Dad you are taking this better than all of us". Randy said, "I am in a win-win situation." He told Garrett, "If I die, I get to go to heaven and be with Jesus. If I get well, I stay here with you and the family." It may be sometime before we all see the "good" in Randy leaving us so early. But we have to know that God has a purpose for that and continue to trust him with the rest of our lives.

Dr. Stallone, a thoracic surgeon, came in and looked over Randy's lab work and said he would like to take the lung and see if he could contain the cancer. However, mesothelioma is such a small cancer that you can't detect it with scans, so he wouldn't know what he was dealing with until he had Randy on the table. So we set a date for surgery.

That surgery day came, and I was on pins and needles. When the surgeon came out and gave us the update on the surgery, I still couldn't comprehend how serious the findings were. All I heard was that he didn't take the lung and so I began jumping up and down in joy. I didn't understand that the reason for not taking the lung was not good.

It's funny how the brain protects you from what you can't process at the time. Even with a friend taking notes, I didn't quite accept it all for a few weeks. In hindsight, taking the lung and having the cancer contained in one area would have been the best situation. I wanted Randy to have both lungs and to be able to breathe easily. It's amazing how little control we have. We think we are the masters of our fate...that we call the shot. But it is so far from the truth.

Important: Have someone write down important details. You may not remember everything you will need later.

Our surgeon was Dr. Stallone at Alta Bates. He was in his seventies during this time, and we found him to be absolutely fabulous. Rumor has it that he was a big game hunter and shot off his big toe, and that's why he walks with a limp. Despite that rumored mishap, he had an excellent reputation. Dr. Sloan, with gorgeous blue eyes, was our anesthesiologist. I loved the way he was on duty and made Randy's pain control a priority. He would appear within moments of being called, even in the middle of the night. Both these doctors felt bad for Randy's plight. I know they were hoping for a better outcome for him. I hope you have doctors like these. They see you for the person you are and give you the best of care. I would recommend either of these doctors for excellent care. I loved that they talked to the person and not the disease.

During this period of being hospital bound, we were showered with meals and rides for the boys. I would come home to find bags of sandwiches from the New Deli, or a crock pot of soup, or a big salad. One day, we even got a big box of fried chicken. My boys were picked up and taken to and from school and karate lessons. I truly will be forever grateful for these people God put in our path to pick up the slack.

Such help is needed since battling such a disease means no one has a set schedule anymore. I remember being so tired one night that I fell asleep at a red light as I got off the freeway. The car behind me honked his horn and woke me up. When I got home, the boys were there alone. Garrett is now 10 and Brady 15, and to top it off, we were out of milk. I thought about running to store, but decided against it. Instead, I made a call, and an "angel" came right over with a gallon. We were surrounded by people who were there to help us. We were so lucky and we knew it.

When school was out, Randy's sister Colleen stayed with us for a week to help out while Randy was recovering from surgery. Randy had come home, but he was in so much pain and so weak and fragile that he could do little. What a tremendous support she was, especially during the holidays while the boys were home. Someone was here with them while I worked. She had gone through this very situation for thirty years with her father, and I am sure she was hoping for better news...like we all were.

Here we are at the end of 2006. What a year!

Here it is right after Christmas and before a New Year. 2006 left us in a wake of adversity, and we were just so happy to get Randy home from his lung surgery. My father was diagnosed as terminal in March, and in April, we had to deal with a five day undiagnosed ruptured appendix with our youngest son. I was so glad to see this year end.

When we walked in the door and got Randy settled, my cousin, Dave, called me into the garage. Our water heater had busted, and we had water all over the place. I was able to call our neighbor who happened to be a plumber.

Stu Love came over and wrote out a list of items to pick up from the hardware store and bring back. So Dave and I went to the local hardware store. I remember being so tired and not being able to process things. I kept thinking, *wasn't this enough? Wasn't getting Randy home enough? Why did the hot water heater have to break too?* We got everything that was on the list, and on New Year's Day, Stu replaced our water heater. It was a gift of love and he refused payment. I would highly recommend Eastshore Plumbing, in Pinole, to anyone. It was the first of many gifts we received during our journey.

Left to Right..
Scott Christensen, Randy, Donny Maestas (Chemosabi),
Brian Christopher, Misi Christopher and Pat Caldie

Chapter 3: January 2007, Beginning Treatment

Actual Copies of Internet Updates

January 3, 2007

We had a three PM appointment today with Dr. Pfister at the Alta Bates Comprehensive Cancer Center. He was our first ray of sunshine. He says he has seen a few people beat this type of cancer. We were told by his associate that there was no cure and was a matter of quality of life. However, it will be a battle. We are going in with our amour. I told Randy I want to keep Dr. Pfister. He's a fighter, and I want a doctor who will always look on the bright side.

We will start chemo on Jan 16th from noon; it will be a five-hour ordeal. Randy has to go back the day after for a booster shot, Nulesta, to get his body to produce more white cells. This process is every three weeks. Therefore it's one chemo treatment every three weeks for six cycles. The last one will be in May.

However, if Randy is up to it, he can go to work in between treatments. This did put a smile on Randy's face. So, today is a good day. We know we have a battle, and we can feel your prayers. Thank you and don't stop praying. I'll keep you updated. Our next doctor's appointment is next Tues, with his surgeon, for a follow up. I know he will just look over Randy's stitches and tell us he is doing great. Thank you so much for the prayers. Debbie…

<u>January 9, 2007</u>

We now have two e-mail groups. One list was getting too big, and the system was rejecting it. So I have A - H in one group and the rest in another. I just wanted to give you another update. We went to see Randy's surgeon today, and he was very pleased with Randy's recovery from surgery. Randy's x-ray was almost normal. He has cleared Randy to go back to work on Thursday, until Tues (1/16) when we start chemo. Randy will take the day of chemo off as well as the day after and work the rest of the time—subject to change if needed. The surgeon said Randy is the healthiest patient with mesothelioma he has ever seen. He also thinks that it is very possible that chemo and radiation could do the trick and we won't need the second surgery at UCSF. We are going with that.

We start chemo on 1/16. I know it's going to be a rough road, but we know we are not on it alone. We have so many blessings through this ordeal; we see God's hand at every turn. The elders from our church are coming over on Friday to pray for us. Thank you for your prayers and encouragement. Debbie…

January 16, 2007

I am giving you the latest update. We just finished our first chemo. It seems, with this type of chemo treatment, the nausea factor should be low. However, we will have some meds on hand just in case. Randy will start to get tired in 8 to 9 days from now. So, right now, he is doing really well. We go tomorrow for a booster shot (to stimulate his bone marrow into making new cells), a checkup next Thursday the 28th, and then we are clear for takeoff until Feb 6th for the next round. As long as Randy is feeling well, he can go to work. I asked the question, "How do we know if the chemo is being effective?" And the answer was, "We don't know." We go through the treatments, do a CAT scan in 6 weeks to 4 months, and see what we can see. There are no "markers" or blood tests. Even with the CAT scans, you can't always see the little tumors. If he is still alive in three years, he's cured. Wow, it's the 21st Century and we are flying by the seat of our pants.

The main thing is that Randy is home and seems to be doing well. We have to keep him eating and his weight up. Please keep us in prayer, and I'll let you know if anything pertinent shows up. In the meantime, we are doing well. Blessings to all, Debbie...

January 18, 2007

Well, things are still a bit crazy around here. Here are three amigos, wearing Sponge Bob shirts. Thought you'd get a kick out of the photo. So far so good, with the chemo; a few side effects and Randy was back on the air this morning, 1100 AM on your radio dial. Or you can go to KFAX.com and get broadcasting online. Keep us in your prayers. Debbie

January 26, 2007

We received some good news yesterday, and I thought I'd share with you. Randy went in for a checkup and his blood count was back to normal. With this chemo treatment, his blood count should have been as low, but it was normal! As you may know, chemo kills all the new dividing cells, and when the mature cells die off, then there are no new cells to replace the dying ones; he should have been tired and anemic. He feels so good. Randy plans to stop by the gym today.

We got a call today from oncology, wanting Randy to come back on Tues 1/30 to discuss treatment options. I don't know what that means. But after yesterday's blood test, there was some discussion, and they want to see Randy next week.

Currently we don't have another chemo session until February 6th. So I am not sure what will be happening this Tuesday. Keep praying for us. We know we are in God's hands. Debbie...

January 31, 2007

Well, just to keep everybody up to speed. Randy is doing really great. The first chemo session is about over and he did really well. He did get nauseated some, and was very tired a few days, but overall, we are happy with how he went through the first session.

We saw Dr. Pfister yesterday, and he wants to add a protein blocker (chemo treatment) to Randy's treatment called Avastin. It's $30,000 per treatment! The insurance doesn't cover it, and it can cause internal bleeding. I've looked it up and can't find a place where it's been used in mesothelioma (it's been used in colon cancer and small cell lung cancer). So I think we are going to wait on that and continue research.

We are also getting a second opinion with Dr. Jahan at UCSF. He is one of the leading specialists in the country for mesothelioma. We are lucky he is across the bay and not across the country—just to make sure we are doing everything we can. We have an appointment on March 5, 2007.

Okay, we are good to go. Next chemo session starts on Feb 6th, 11:30 AM. Now we know what to expect; it isn't as scary. Thank you so much for cards, phone calls, food, books, and information. We feel loved. Blessings, Debbie & Randy...

Debbie's Thoughts

As I walked into the cancer center, it was hard to put one foot in front of the other. _Why are we here? This can't be our fate._ I didn't want to walk in. I wanted to run and run fast and hard away from that place. Randy was so healthy! What happened? I felt like I was in a fog, a deer in the headlights. Everybody was so kind, encouraging and supportive. I didn't care. I just wanted out. I couldn't catch my breath.

Randy kept assuring me that this was the place for him to get better. Randy was emotionally stronger than I was. He was the one that was so sick, and I was the one falling apart, inside and outside. I kept thinking I was in a dream and would wake up. It was so overwhelming. I just couldn't believe it was real. It just had to be a dream. _When am I going to wake up from this nightmare?_

Looking back, I realize how often the resident psychologist would "just turn up" and sit with me for a while. I guess I was looking a bit overwhelmed or crying, and someone would "turn me in." I think having a distraught person in the waiting room would start everybody crying.

We were at Alta Bates Comprehensive Cancer Center and every person there was fabulous, from the parking attendants, the nurses, and the receptionists to the doctors. Randy received the best treatments there. Randy just took it all in stride, went where they told him to, but would pass out whenever a needle would come by. He did get better with that.

Very shortly after Randy's surgery, some of God's mighty warriors from Community Alliance Church in Richmond, eight of them, came over and laid hands on Randy and prayed. The boys and I were included. We gathered around in our family room and prayed for healing, God's leading, and for wisdom. It was such a comfort to be surrounded by love. We wanted God's hand on us, and we wanted to be obedient to His Word. God met us there that day and every day after.

Is any one of you sick? He should call the elders of the church to pray over him and anoint him with oil in the name of the Lord. – **James 5:14**

Like others in our situation, we wanted to make sure we were doing everything we could on every available front. We had prayer being offered up and we had the medical world doing all they could, so we also began looking into alterative and natural remedies. There are so many homeopathic alternatives out there that it could be overwhelming. Indeed, you need to be wise about what you chose to use.

We were bombarded by alternative treatment plans that caring and loving people tried to share with us. We had one testimonial which really looked believable. It was a very expensive nutrition drink that supposedly *cures mesothelioma*! The lady who was "cured" had her blood marker count go down. This is very interesting, because there are *no blood markers* for mesothelioma at this time. In order to check on the cancer, Randy has to have a PET scan. So that story about that woman was not true. Another treatment was a coffee enema, but Randy decided he liked his coffee going down the other end of his body. I told Randy to check them all out and decide what treatment he wanted to do.

So beware! Take a look at what is being offered, take it to the doctor, and do your own research. What homeopathic treatment may work for one cancer *may help another cancer thrive*. Cancer is a big money maker. People are desperate, looking for a cure, anything. And people know that you would empty your bank accounts, sell your house, your valuables, your pets, anything. You could end up worse off than if you had done nothing—so research, research, research. If you don't have a computer, find someone who does—one of those people who say, "Call me if you need anything." Call them and say, "Can you look up vitamin B6 and my cancer and see what it says?" Or ask, "Does juicing carrots and veggies really help my type of cancer, or does the sugar in them make it grow faster?" Juicing might be a good way to go, but only if you pair it up with a protein. You really are willing to do anything, so check things out, no matter how harmless things may seem to look like.

Recently, a friend of mine gave his wife LDN for her breast cancer. Her four sisters were all in remission from breast cancer by using LDN. Some have found that in small doses it has been very successful in breast cancer and MS treatments. Her sisters pleaded with him to try it on his wife because she was declining so fast. So, against her doctor's advice and his better judgment, he bought some off the internet and gave her a very small dose. It interacted negatively with her pain meds and she ended up in the emergency room. When I got to the hospital, they had to sedate her to control her pain.

LDN removes all narcotics out of the blood stream. Since the cancer had gone into her bones, she had been taking heavy doses of pain medications for many months. The instant removal of her pain meds put her into a seizure. Therefore, even if your family and friends are giving you proven advice, it may be wise to double check with the doctor. If the doctor discourages the advice, find out why. Don't be afraid to ask lots of questions. You don't want to live with a regret you don't have to. It took a couple of days, but my friend recovered, and they got her pain back under control.

Shortly after Randy's surgery and after we started chemo, I received a note from an old boss of mine living in Southern California. He had sent a card and a gift of $500.00. He told me that he thought we would need it. I immediately sent a thank you note. The very next day, a bill from Dr. Sloan's office, Mr. "Dr. Blue Eyes," came for $517.00! I wasn't expecting a bill. Randy had never really gotten sick before and I wasn't expecting co-pays, deductibles, out of network bills, and other expenses. The insurance the boys and I had worked differently. I hadn't even given insurance a thought! But God was telling us that He was taking care of us. It really was a blessing. Before we knew we would have a need, God provided. He would prove His faithfulness to us over and over again.

When Randy got sick, we didn't have a savings. Even with health insurance, there were so many deductibles and co-pays and out of network payments that money became a major issue. We had anywhere from eight to ten thousand a year in out of pocket expenses. The cost for 20% of cancer treatment is a lot of money. However, when Randy passed away, we were not in debt. All of our bills were *"somehow"* covered. That is God's faithfulness! There are so many amazing stories of God's provision in this story! I figured almost $25,000 in gifts was given to us in the 32 months of Randy's illness, mostly from wonderful friends and some anonymous givers. After his death, I was able to pay forward all the gifts given to us and then some. Since we were given so much, I asked the recipients not to pay me back, but when their circumstances changed, to pay forward the gift given to someone else in need. This way, the kindness that was shown to us will grow in future years and hopefully make the world a better place for it.

"Before you call, I will answer; while you are still speaking, I will hear." – Isaiah 65:24

At this time, there were four specialists on mesothelioma in the country. We were so lucky to have one over the bridge and not across the country. Dr. Jahan, at UCSF Comprehensive Cancer Center in San Francisco, is also doing research studies on mesothelioma. I would recommend him in a heartbeat for mesothelioma care. His own father had passed from this particular cancer, so he has a vested interested in seeing something work.

We were truly blessed to find a mesothelioma legal advocate, Kazan Law Office, in Oakland. Steven Kazan fought hard for Randy's care and rights, as he had done for Randy's father before him. Randy is a second generation asbestos victim. Steven Kazan has been fighting for cancer patient's rights for over 30 years. The Kazan Law Firm also supports cancer research at UCSF, which spoke loudly to our hearts. They were in the trenches with us, helping to find a cure. When we walked into the University Of California San Francisco Cancer Center, we saw Kazan's name on the wall of honored donors. Not only was Kazan's firm on top of all the latest laws concerning asbestos, they also knew where one of the most comprehensive health care centers for mesothelioma was located. Kazan's office helped me get the appointment with Dr. Jahan at UCSF, when it was so difficult. They continued to open doors for us to get the fastest research and appointments all throughout Randy's illness. I called on them many times for help, and they were very knowledgeable about the disease and how to find treatment. How wonderful to have a pit bull at your side when you need to take a bite out of cancer. We are indebted to the whole Kazan staff for their knowledge and care.

Chapter 4: February 2007

Treatments and Blessings

Actual Copies of Internet Updates

February 6, 2007

We went in for the second session of chemo today. Everything went really well. Blood tests are normal and Randy took the IV, without too much of a problem. I don't know if you know, but sometimes Randy passes out when someone comes at him with a needle.

I did do some research on Avastin, but Jeri, who is an oncology nurse, really explained it well below:

Avastin is being used more and more in the fight against cancer these days. It was released a couple of years ago and the clinical trials proposed its use for metastatic colon cancer. However, since then it has been used in addition to standard chemo for lung and now is being considered for breast as well. Avastin cuts off the expression of VEGF, which is the normal chemical in our bodies that causes blood vessels to grow. So...when a tumor grows enough to tap into the blood vessels surrounding it for its supply of nutrients, the Avastin cuts off that supply. Since it makes sense to cut off the blood supply to any tumor, it is being studied for many cancers presently. It cannot be used on anyone that has had surgery within 30 days or a lung cancer patient with bloody hemoptysis (coughing up blood) and is used with monitoring of urine, blood counts, evidence of GI bleed, etc. It also isn't appropriate for anyone with history of MI (heart attack). So, I'm sure your oncologist has thought it through. As with any chemo, there is risk involved, but that's why the doc and nurses follow the patients so closely. The second opinion is always useful, primarily because it usually reinforces what it already being done. Oncologists throughout the Bay Area seem to stay in touch with each other and usually submit the less common cases (such as Randy's) to a "tumor board" which is a multi-disciplinary group of docs, radiologists, nurses, managers, etc. that go over the case presented and discuss all the possibilities. They also keep in contact from one hospital to another exchanging info, ideas, etc. I'm sure Randy is in good hands. Jeri...

Hi Jeri,

I did call Genentech in San Francisco, the manufacture of Avastin, and spoke to a pharmaceutical researcher there about the clinical trials. Avastin is *not* FDA approved for mesothelioma at this time. We spoke to Dr. Pfister (Alta Bates) and he said we could discuss it further at UCSF. Dr. Pfister is going to meet with the specialist at UCSF next week to go over Randy's case and order our PET or CAT scan (whichever UCSF wants) for our meeting on March 5th. The specialist at UCSF wants three chemo treatments before he sees Randy.

Randy goes in for his Nulesta shot (boosts blood cells) tomorrow and we are good to go until 2/27. We are hoping that Randy responds well to this treatment as he did the first. However, we know it could be a bit more taxing. Randy wants to work through this treatment.

Keep us in your prayers. God is good and He has been good to us. Your prayers sustain us. Blessings, Debbie…

February 28, 2007

We had our third chemo treatment…three more to go. The nurse had a hard time finding a vein, so it took a few tries to get in an IV. Good thing we had him lying down. Good thing she believed me when I told her we had a fainter.

We have a CT scan scheduled for tomorrow. It was requested for our second consult with UCSF on Monday, March 5th. Truly I feel we are on the right track doing everything that possibly can be done at this time. We are still looking for your prayers. I'll update again after our UCSF appointment. Blessings, Debbie…

March 5, 2007

Hello everybody,

We had our second opinion at UCSF with Dr. Jahan today. We took in a CT scan that we had done last week. Based on the CT scan and the exam, the doctor (mesothelioma oncologist) feels that the chemo is doing a great job. He said it made him happy to see it.

We are in stage two maybe stage three at this time. The chemo and radiation will only slow down the progress of the mesothelioma and, right now, buy us one to three years.

However, Randy is in good shape, young, the chemo seems to be doing a great job, and Randy may be a candidate for the second surgery. We need a PET scan and meet with a surgeon at UCSF. The doctor feels that the surgery would buy us more time and maybe even cure the cancer, maybe—a big maybe.

Randy has done his own research on the surgery and has reservations about this. We

54

have decided to push through the PET scan and meet with the surgeon and get all the facts and make an educated decision, hopefully, before the next chemo treatment of March 20th. The decision to have surgery will be Randy's.

The surgery would entail taking the lining of the heart and diaphragm, removing the left lung and part of the esophagus. Recovery time is six to 12 months. Once the doctors feel that he is up to it, he will resume his chemo treatments and radiation.

It's a lot to think about and process. We appreciate the prayers. I know God is with us. I have no doubt. We are in His care and I know He will lead us. Blessings to you all, Debbie...

Debbie's Thoughts

I have found comfort in the tapes of Randy's shows and some of the interviews he had done on the air before he died. I'll be sharing them from time to time in the book. Here is another one:

February 2007, Spirit of Praise (Radio program):

"This is 1100 AM, Spirit of Praise. I'm Randy Brady. Recently, I had some surgery, and when I got out of the hospital, some friends

came over to visit me. And we kind of got into a discussion about why bad things happen to good people. Not that I am a good person; frankly I think bad things happen to good people, because there are no good people. We have all sinned.

"But in other countries, people know that life is hard and they turn to God for help. But in the United States, we tend to think, well, we are entitled to life, liberty and not only the pursuit of happiness, but happiness itself. So when bad things happen, a lot of times we get mad at God and we think there is an injustice here and we turn away from the only one with the answers, the only one who can help." – Randy Brady

I will lift my eyes to the mountains; from whence shall my help come? My help comes from the Lord, Who made heaven and earth. He will not allow your foot to slip; He who keeps you when you slumber. Behold, He who keeps Israel, will neither slumber nor sleep. – Psalm 121:1-4

Many nights, I found myself unable to sleep and only by singing praise songs could I sing myself to sleep. I would wake up in the middle of the night and say, "Oh, it's only a dream," and then I realized that Randy was really sick and this was my reality. God reminded me that even though these were scary times, I could find comfort in Him. He is a part of the good times and the bad. By building my life on "The Rock" over the years, the storms may blow, but God, Himself, would keep me anchored.

He is like a man building a house, which dug down deep and laid the foundation on rock. When a flood came, the torrent struck that house but could not shake it, because it was well built. – Matthew 6:48

Maybe you share a similar reality now. You are in this boat, not sure what tomorrow may bring. Which way to turn? My advice is to just get through today. Sometimes you can only deal with this hour. It's okay. It's hard and scary. Just take today. Wake up tomorrow and deal with tomorrow then. If you look at the bigger picture, it does get overwhelming.

As for me, I couldn't take antidepressants to cope. My stomach wouldn't tolerate it, making me sick. So I would have to deal head on with daily panic attacks. To help, I used a counting system. I would count to five breathing in, count to five holding it in, and then count to five while breathing it out. I also recommend talking to God, your pastor, to family and friends. If you don't have friends to talk to, find a neighbor, go to a coffee shop, find someone sitting by themselves and say, "I'm having a hard time, can I talk to you? Will you listen to me for a minute?" You have to talk. You really do, even if it is a stranger. Keep talking or you'll explode or bring it inward, which can turn into depression. I know it gets old and family gets tired of hearing it, but you must keep talking or depression and fear can kick in. Let your family and friends know how important it is to you that these burdens must be shared. You are not meant to carry the load alone.

"Two are better than one, because they have a good return for their work: If one falls down, his friend can help him up." – Ecclesiastes 4: 9-10

For *"Whoever will call on the name of the Lord will be saved."* – Romans 10:13 (NASB)

If you are reading this and you have a friend or family member going through terminal cancer or grieving the loss of a loved one, the best thing you can do is listen to them—to be there when they need you and to hear them work out their pain and not to turn them away into their loneliness and grief, which can turn into despair and helplessness.

Yes, there are counselors, but it takes years to get to know someone. A counselor won't know the family dynamics like you, the friend, does. You might feel that you don't have any answers or can't fix the problem, but that isn't your job. Here is some insight: counselors can't fix this either. God is the healer, so you are off the hook. You don't have to fix it…how can you? God will. You just have to listen and be there in any way you can.

Maybe go over for coffee or go out to breakfast, bring over a flower, a movie, and a muffin, say a prayer…but most importantly, just listen. They need to know someone is there, that they are loved, included and part of a family. Don't let a long time go by without calling and checking up on them. They may vent on you, but this is part of the healing process. The anger is not directed at you; they are angry at the cancer, fear, or death. They need someone strong to hold on to. They need someone—they need you! Don't shy or go away. Stand up, be strong, and be the family or friend they need and can count on.

One day, this may be you going through a hard time, and won't it be wonderful to have a friend in your pocket who completely understands?

Let us not lose heart in doing good, for in due time we will reap if we do not grow weary. – Galatians 6:9 (NASB)

If you are a caregiver, it's important to take care of yourself. So much responsibility is placed on your shoulders. One way is to exercise. Get out and walk or go to the gym. This was so helpful in allowing me to release tension, anxiety and stress hormones. It will help you breathe and relax. You read that and hesitate, no doubt thinking of all the things you have to get done. But guess what? They will still be there when you get back, but you will be in a better frame of mind and can think clearer. The chores will get done faster after a good workout. At one point, me and my boys bought a treadmill and walked while Randy was recovering from a chemo treatment. I worried about what the boys would have to deal with if I was out of the house, so I brought the workout home.

I also spent some time in prayer and meditation. Just praying, taking some time with just me and God, just giving Him some of my problems so I didn't have to hold on to each one, was a big help. When I did that, it was amazing how each thing fell into place. Doors opened up. When the situation was difficult, I wasn't. Now don't get me wrong. There were days I was difficult or as some say, "high maintenance," especially dealing with the insurance companies and trying to get pain medications.

Speaking of help, when someone would say, "If you need help, call me," I did! I would ask for rides to get my kids home from school, karate, and events. I'd ask for things I needed from the grocery store. I'd ask for medications when I or the kids were sick. I put out the calls when I needed to.

Dealing with everything is so exhausting. I remember one day after coming home from a busy day and Randy was resting from a treatment. I was finishing up dishes when Randy asked, "Why is Jim bringing Brady home from karate? Can't you go get him?"

I paused, feeling utterly wiped out. I had been on the go for so long and for so many days. Finally I said, "Because I can't do it all, all the time. I am so drained."

Jim's help may seem like a little thing, but it meant so much. It was so nice to have a night where I didn't have to go back out at nine to pick up my son and bring him home. I was already struggling with panic attacks from all the things I was juggling. If someone offers to help, call them. I did.

One of the things we chose to focus on was life. Even though Randy had a terminal diagnosis—Randy always said that we all die eventually—I knew that as long as Randy had breath, God could heal him. I have seen, with my own eyes, God's mighty healing. I have laid hands and prayed on an 81 year-old woman who was in a comma from being hit by a car and God raised her up even after the doctors had given up. She lived for another twelve years after that. A few weeks after my prayer for her, I had the pleasure of praying with her daughter to receive Christ as her Savior. I have laid hands on and prayed and seen God remove breast cancer left over from a failed surgery. I knew if God chose to, He could also heal Randy at any time. God can do amazing things. I have witnessed this first hand. God didn't heal everybody we prayed for, but sometimes He did. So we lived each day with the hope of God's healing touch.

So everyday Randy woke up, we lived that day to the fullest.

However, we started getting distressful calls to the house from people who wanted to focus more on Randy's impending death. Some thought we were in denial and not properly preparing for his passing, but how could they know that? Nothing ticked me off more than people focused on the "death sentence" and who wanted to share their concerns with us. Oh gosh, really? They wanted us to focus on his death and we wanted to focus on life!

Later, in the email updates, you'll see I asked people not to call the house unless they had something positive to say. People we hadn't seen or heard from in twenty years were calling the house, crying because Randy was dying any day! This was particularly upsetting to our two boys who could hear the conversation. This is why I started the email updates. Getting those calls was terribly cruel. I think if you know someone who has a health issue, which could be terminal, you might consider *sending an encouraging call or note*, instead of reminding them of the problem. Please reconsider writing or calling to say, "Good-bye, see you on the other side." Frankly, that is not encouraging to someone who is looking for courage every day to fight to live. It was such a discouragement to Randy and the rest of us to get those types of calls and letters.

In the words of Patrick Swayze's doctor when commenting on the tabloids' exploitation of Swayze's health condition, "It is emotional cruelty." I whole heartily second that opinion. I believe that these people would never do anything "intentionally" to hurt us. They just didn't realize how their calls and notes were affecting us. So unless someone calls and says, "Hey, I'm calling to say goodbye," don't go there. You might want to try, "Hello, how are you today?"

Saying goodbye is for memorial services and funerals, not to a living breathing person. Randy lived thirty-two months after his diagnosis. Can you imagine hearing about how bad people feel about your "death sentence" for that long? That would have been 960 days of doom and gloom. We had living to do. I got to the point, after taking so many of those calls, that I just started handing the phone to Randy. Actually, in retrospect, I should have hung up the phone and thrown out the messages. It was way more then we could handle on top of the treatments. At one point, I would scan notes and letters first before giving them to Randy. When I did give him one, I would say, "This is safe to read." He would thank me. In our house, we tried to keep things as normal as possible. We hoped that such a plan would squelch the rumors of his impending death and prevent more of those phone calls.

I bring this up as both a warning and a caution. This caused additional stress to the whole family, especially our boys who were already scared to death that their dad was dying. Those boys heard over and over again about Randy's dying. Imagine how they felt. Randy and I found it very discouraging as we fought every day keep him alive. I know people don't know what to say in difficult situations. However, an alternative is, "I hope you get well and I'm praying for you." Better yet, ask, **"How can I help?"**

One day there was a knock on my door by a lovely lady from the church. We went to a fairly large church. Though I recognized her, I didn't really ever remember having a conversation with this gal before. But Randy has been up front and active in the church, so she knew of us and probably felt like more than an acquaintance. She seemed like a very nice lady. I don't know who she had been talking with, but she was very concerned that I wasn't facing reality. She came to the house to share her concerns in person. Wow, that was odd...and awkward. So I said, "We were recently at the cemetery picking out a plot and at the funeral home picking out a casket. Is that facing reality enough?" Of course she was flabbergasted, not knowing any of that. Why would she? We didn't know her and she wasn't family.

What I didn't tell her was that Randy dragged me the memorial grounds kicking, screaming, and crying. I kept saying, "If we do this, does this mean we don't have enough faith that God is going to heal you?"

His answer was, "I'm going to die and it is 100% certain. It may be fifty years from now, or two, but it's best to be prepared." Our family didn't even know we had gone to make these arrangements. I am happy to say that this woman and her husband later became such big supporters and encouragers. God used them both in a mighty way to let me know how powerful the Lord was in my life. One day, after returning home completely exhausted and not having any time to prepare a meal, they knocked on our door and said, "God told us you needed a chicken!" What a great meal.

Another day, I had a brake light out on the van. I had purchased the replacement light, but was dealing with a raging migraine and just didn't feel I had the energy to replace it. I was driving up the hill to my house and saw this dear couple following me home. They had bought us some veggies and other goodies and were coming over to deliver them. Her husband replaced the brake light for me. They really did step up to the plate. Even after Randy passed, they continued to bless me and the boys. They turned out to be one of our best blessings. Things just started out a little odd.

Rejoice in the Lord always. I will say it again: Rejoice! Let your gentleness be evident to all. The Lord is near. Do not be anxious about anything, but in everything, by prayer and petition, with thanksgiving, present your requests to God. And the peace of God, which transcends all understanding, will guard your hearts and your minds in Christ Jesus. Finally, brothers, whatever is true, whatever is noble, whatever is right, whatever is pure, whatever is lovely, whatever is admirable--if anything is excellent or praiseworthy--think about such things. Whatever you have learned or received or heard from me, or seen in me--put it into practice. And the God of peace will be with you. – Philippians 4:4-9

Chapter 5: Spring, Summer, and Fall of 2007—Easy Breezy

March 20, 2007

Hey everybody, we had our fourth chemo session today. So far things are going well. Randy is now taking a nap. We were at the cancer center all day, and I'm tired. The third chemo session went really well. We were pleased that every hair on his head stayed in place. We are hoping that this session goes as well.

Randy hopes to be back on the air tomorrow.

Thank you for all your phone calls. I know people want to know what is going on, so I hope this answers your questions.

We asked his oncologist at Alta Bates (Dr. Pfister) about the radical pneumonectomy surgery at UCSF, and he does recommend that Randy do it. We are not sure if the surgery will really buy us more "quality" time. We will investigate it closely. It's a very radical surgery. Randy really is leaning against it. He is willing to give the surgeons a chance to talk him into it.

65

So we have a PET scan scheduled for Friday in San Francisco and an appointment for a consultation with the surgeon on April 6th. I'll follow up after the surgeon's appointment.

On Sunday evening, we are planning to go to Vacaville for a prayer service. A good friend, Laurie, really recommends these guys. Let us know if you want to come. Debbie…

April 5, 2007

Hi everybody,

I've gotten a few calls and emails asking how Randy is…they hadn't heard anything for a while. So I thought I'd send an update. Praise the Lord; no news is good news!

Just to let you guys know, Randy is getting over the fifth chemo treatment and is doing phenomenally well! This time around was better than the fourth treatment. We have one more treatment on May 1st. We also know that the chemo is doing its job and is really keeping the cancer growth down. The chemo can't kill the cancer on a molecular scale, but God can. After Randy recovers from chemo, we will start radiation. When I know more about radiation, I'll let you know.

We are off to Bodega Bay for the weekend. Randy's sister is taking our boys up to Ukiah for a time of torture with Uncle John. Brady & Garrett are getting their arsenal together. Colleen has asked for medical release papers. All kidding aside, they have a great time with their Uncle John. It's wacky and crazy and they come back exhausted.

We are in God's hands and your prayers! Please keep praying for us when God brings us to your hearts and minds. Thank you so much for your love, encouragement, and support. It means more to us then you'll ever know. Your prayers have made an extremely difficult situation bearable. Blessings, Debbie…

May 24, 2007

Hi guys,

We had a meeting with the doctor of radiation at Alta Bates Cancer Center early Tuesday morning. Dr. Swift seems very likable and interviewed Randy and his concerns extensively. He said Randy looked like a "million bucks" and he does! Right now his quality of life is good. We discussed the radiation and what needs to be done. Right now Randy isn't in pain and doesn't have any difficulty breathing. So that is a good sign. Dr.

67

Swift says they start treatment when there are difficulties.

Dr. Swift wanted to discuss Randy's case with the two specialists we saw at UCSF and look at all the scans and then present to us in a week or so. He did tell us that Randy needed radiation for about 1/2 hour a day for six weeks and that there are four areas of concern:

One, there can be spinal cord damage. However, that should be minimal, if any. Two, the esophagus will be burned and it may be difficult to eat for three or four weeks, but the tissue will heal. Randy is putting on extra weight in advance for this. Three, the lung tissue doesn't like radiation and it is very likely that he will lose the use of his left lung permanently. Four, is his heart; once they radiate his heart, it will be weakened.

I'll update you all in a week or so after Dr. Swift makes his presentation. Since Randy is doing so well, it's my hope we hold off on the radiation and let him enjoy this quality of life. Who knows, maybe for a long time we can enjoy life. Keep us in prayer; we see God working every day. Blessings, Debbie…

June 15, 2007

It's amazing! We have good news to rejoice! Randy met with the Radiologist Oncologist, Dr. Swift, yesterday and he said we can wait for radiation! Randy is doing so well that radiation will bring down his quality of life. His left lung functions and heart will be compromised. So he wants to wait until Randy isn't doing so well, and then radiate him so he is better.

Randy is doing so well, you wouldn't have a clue he has cancer. Not a clue! His color, his weight, his energy levels are all really good! It is truly amazing.

We don't have another appointment until September 4th for a checkup. Yippee! If we can go this way for three months or three years, it will be fine with me. We are still in God's hands and your prayers.

On a different note, I had my own mishap on June 1st. I have suffered with migraines for over 15 years. Well, did you know you can pass out with a migraine? I had just taken Garrett to school and walked in the door. I was nauseated, looking for my medication and thought, "I'm going to pass out." Well I did and my head hit the fireplace and the fireplace won. However, I did chip a brick in my defense.

I don't remember, but I ended up in the hospital with seven staples in the back of my head. I didn't even know why I was there, how I got there. I just know I had a migraine and they wouldn't give me any medication for it. When we got home, we saw all the blood on the floor and my glasses on the fireplace and carpet. Not until then did I know why I was in the hospital. I see a neurologist today to get my head examined. This should make some of my family members and friends very happy.

I wasn't scared. I didn't even know what was happening. My thinking cleared up yesterday. I feel like I can think straight. I am remembering things again. I'm still slurring my words. That might be the booze talking (only kidding). In spite of these situations, I know we are blessed. Both our situations could be different. I know God is in control and we are hanging on tight to Him.

We are planning a trip to Hawaii. Randy wants to take the boys to Oahu and take them to different places and we want to do it while Randy is in such great shape. I probably won't update you again until September 4th, unless something happens. I think we're good to go. Please come and visit, drop by, say hello. We want to celebrate every day we have. Blessings to you all; thank you so much for your love, support, cards, letters, encouragement…we know we are not alone. Debbie…

The good news is Randy is still doing very well. He out-hiked me everywhere in Hawaii. He is really doing well. We have our next checkup on 9/4. I hope the doctors send him back out again without treatments. That would be wonderful. We had a spectacular time in Hawaii. I did delay the takeoff by an hour because I saw what looked like a hole in the plane's window. I showed the stewardess, the pilot came out, than the maintenance crew came out, than they came in, took the window out, and found that what looked like a hole was a bubble inside the glass. Who knew? I did move Garrett and myself to another section of the plane.

Once in Hawaii, we hiked to Wiamiea Falls, snorkeled in Hanama Bay, Randy and Brady went to Pearl Harbor. We swam with the sea turtles in the ocean right by our hotel. If you look at the photo of Randy and me on the balcony, three sea turtles make their home in the water behind us. We had rumors of Hurricane Flossy, had a big fire, and an earthquake. My uncle wanted to know what I was doing over there. I said, "I am moving and shaking things up!" We just loved it. Thank you for your continued support and prayers. I'll send another update when we hear what the doctors have to say after our appointment. Blessings, Debbie.

September 4, 2007

Randy just saw Dr. Pfister this afternoon and had a blood test and checkup. Dr. Pfister said, "See you in about three months!" Randy has to get a PET scan before going back, but praise the Lord! I really didn't want to go back to that cancer center. Yes, I know it's a great place to get help, but I just didn't want to go back. Radiation? What radiation? Yeah! Whew!

Thank you so much for your prayers. We are soooo happy! So I guess we'll go back before Thanksgiving for another "checkup." Blessings to all of you, Randy & Debbie...

Debbie's Thoughts

In March, Randy and I were treated to a wonderful time at Bodega Bay. Randy's brother-in-law's brother, Charlie (did you follow that?), had a cabin he lent to us by the water. It was wonderful to get away. The boys went to Ukiah to stay with Randy's sister Colleen and her husband John. They love the boys so much and the boys have such a great time. Colleen had a menu printed for the boys so they knew what they were going to eat. How cute was that? John, of course, would get ready for war when the boys came up. It could be water balloons, silly string, frogs, anything he can throw at them, literally. My boys start planning an arsenal of their own and get their suitcases packed for action. John lost three fingers due to saws getting in the way of his hand. One Halloween, we picked up some plastic fingers we found at a store and mailed them to him. We thought he could use a spare.

This was a fantastic summer. Randy finished his first chemo treatment without too much of a struggle. He did get some flu-like symptoms, but he got over them rather quickly. Things at home ran normally for the most part, except me having a fight with the fireplace and leaving me with seven battle stitches in my head. There were a few days that I needed to get boys some rides, but overall the kids had a normal summer of swimming, playing with friends, and conquering video games. I had my twin nephews down for a week. Brady had his friend Patrick stay a week. It was great summer.

We never really took a vacation with our boys. Our lifestyle was one of just paying off bills and keeping things simple. Our vacations depended upon using frequent flier tickets and seeing family in New York or Washington or driving the van up to Washington. Since we didn't have any finances for the trip to Hawaii, I was going to charge it and figure out how to pay it later.

I had never charged anything I couldn't pay off, except the house and cars. I knew I had a lifetime to work, but maybe only a short time with Randy. With Randy's current job at KFAX and me having to work part time to take care of the boys, we didn't have a lot of money. Randy and I felt that making sure the boys were being taken care of was the priority.

Lo and behold, a very big surprise came in the mail. Another good friend sent a check big enough to cover the airfare and hotel. The note included said, "We found Hawaii very healing; go have a good time." To this day, I am very grateful. I was so stunned and very surprised I just sat down and cried. Then another good friend wanted us to attend a luau, so he insisted in treating us to a Hawaiian event. Whenever I think of this trip, I think of how blessed we were. The hotel we stayed out, Outrigger Reef, upgraded us to an ocean front room, due to some construction issues.

While swimming in front of the hotel, a group of three turtles decided to grace us with their presence. It was at first very shocking, thinking a diver was coming out of the water in a wet suit, but wearing the austere face of a big turtle. We started paddling to shore very fast, trying to comprehend what we just witnessed.

While hiking up to Wiamiea Falls, I heard my name being called. I looked up and we were surprised to see Don and Jeanie. We found long time good friends there in the remote part of the island. Only God could put us together like that. It was amazing. Thank you every one who had a part in making that trip for us at that time. It was priceless.

One of the true blessings to us during this time was my Monday Morning Bible study group. I had been a part of this group for over twelve years. Once we started up chemo treatments, one of the members of the group, Judy, started lining up dinners for Tuesday nights or whenever we had chemo or surgery scheduled. This was a group of eight women who had my back through Garrett's ruptured appendix and now Randy's cancer. These women held me and the family up in prayer for every treatment, surgery, procedure, and sickness we went through. They also organized the memorial service as Robbie had a wonderful plan for the reception.

These women still meet and pray. They are true godly women after God's own heart. Joyce was a nurse and came to the hospital and took notes for me when I was too emotionally drained to think straight. Kathie's husband, Rich, gave Randy rides to KFAX and to the cancer center. Kathie spent a night with us while the boys were at camp to help me administer Randy's medication. Judy's brother, we called him, "Uncle Buddy," would jump in with bags and bags of cookies for the boys. What a gift of love that was. Uncle Buddy would soon fight his own battle with terminal cancer, and I must say he fought with all the grace and determination that Randy did. Judy's daughters, who didn't know us, but only knew of us, came and cleaned our house for us one morning, and one of them even knew how to make up a "hospital bed!" How lucky we were to have them in our lives. I know that they were not in my life by accident. True gifts and acts of amazing love and grace I will hold in my heart forever.

Spirit of Praise Radio Show:

"This is Spirit of Praise 1100 AM KFAX. The Spirit of the Bay—that's Jars of Clay, 'God will lift up your Head.' I am Randy Brady and I can attest to that. God will lift up your head, especially in tough times. Maybe you've heard me mentioned that I've recently been diagnosed with lung cancer. When my wife and I told my boys about it, I told them, 'Watch and see how God loves us and how He will show

His love through His people. We are going to get a lot of support, a lot of visitors, and cards and stuff. People will be bringing us food and helping us out. That is God's way, one of His ways, of showing how much He loves us.' Well, I expected a certain amount of it, but I've just been overwhelmed. Our family has been overwhelmed with the love that has been shown to us. It's just been incredible, people bringing us food and offering to help, and really doing it as well. Giving us rides and giving our kids rides to places and things. And prayer, coming over to pray for us, sending cards saying they are praying for us, it's just been incredible. To know that old friends, new friends, and even people I have not met are praying for me…it has given me such strength as my name is passed along to various church prayer lists. So many people are praying for me. And I want you to know, I really appreciate it. Well, more then you'll ever know." - Randy Brady

Chapter 6: Winter 2007—Getting a Port

Actual Copies of Internet Updates

November 9, 2007

Hi guys,

I must say, I've enjoyed our four months off from treatments. It's been so nice to spend time with friends & family. We had a wonderful trip to Hawaii. All in all, we learned we are living the life God has called us to live. Randy doesn't want to change anything.

We did meet with the oncologist yesterday. He went over a PET scan we had done last Friday, 11/2. There have been some changes. The cancer has progressed. Randy has a few new tumors in his left lung, and found some cancer in a few lymph nodes. They are the mediastinal (between the lungs) and the hilar (bronchial area) lymph nodes. Dr. Pfister is starting Randy on a weekly chemo treatment starting Tuesday. This is to continue until we do another PET scan in a few months to see how the treatment is working.

We are hoping he will be able to continue to work at KFAX through this. If you want to hear him by internet, go to KFAX.com and you can pipe in the station. He has a "Spirit of Praise" show that airs on Sundays, noon to two, Pacific Time. Randy handled his last chemo treatments with strength and stamina, and we know God will give him the courage to do it again.

Well, here we are, standing in the need of prayer. We've been so grateful for your support and encouragement. We've seen God deliver us so many times through this ordeal, and we trust He will deliver us again. I'll keep the updates more frequent then I have in the past few months. As always, in your prayers and God's grace...Debbie...

November 14, 2007

Hi guys,

Well, we had a day yesterday. Randy became a pin cushion as they tried five times to start an IV for his chemo. They couldn't get one started, so he didn't have a treatment yesterday. The staff just loves him. They were happy to see him and yet not. They said they have their favorite patients and he is one of them.

We'll have to go in for a port. A device they will put in his chest for IV's and blood drawing. Randy isn't happy about this at all. He will have to miss a day of work, but it will make his treatments a bit easier. He's worried someone will make a mistake putting it in, that it will get infected. However, lots of people get them, and it will be okay. All in all, Randy does really look good. If you didn't know, you wouldn't have a clue. Here's looking for better days to come and a miracle. Blessings, Debbie...

November 28, 2007

Hello everybody,

Thought I'd give you all an update on the latest happenings. Last Monday we were successful in getting a port into Randy. It looks like a doorbell under his skin. The line goes right into a major artery.

Last Tuesday, we had the first chemo treatment and it went smooth. The port really made a big difference! This chemo (Navelbine) isn't wiping him out as much as the chemo we had earlier this year (Alitma).

His treatment plans are three weeks on, one week off. Randy had successful treatments on Nov. 20 & 27, one more on Dec. 4th, then off the week of the 10th, then back onto a schedule.

Randy continues to make it into Fremont to the radio station, 45 miles one way. He then comes home to rest up, eat, sleep and get up and go another day. I am so thankful that he has a job he loves. It's his "purpose" to keep living and fighting. We thank you for your prayers.

We are still looking for a miracle. Until then, we remain in your prayers and God's grace. Blessings, Debbie...

December 5, 2007

As I sit and try and compose this letter, I'm exhausted. I tried to think of the best word to describe yesterday and the word "challenging" comes to mind. Most of the time, I'm up for a good challenge. I grew up with four brothers—I can handle anything!

It started at 4 AM with a migraine. Got Brady off to the bus stop by 6:30, came home, and had to take something for the headache. So my good friend, Lynda, came to the rescue and got Garrett off to school.

Then Randy came home early from work. He has had some pain in his back since surgery and has been taking Tylenol for it until this past month...he's stepped up, taking some Vicodin for it. So he took a Vicodin and rested. Then we were off to a chemo treatment where he passed out when they did his blood draw. After they got Randy settled in a bed, I called to check on the boys. Garrett's ride home forgot him, and at four, he was still at the school waiting for a pick up. It just so happened we have a good friend, Cynthia, working there and she brought Garrett home for us. Sometimes I feel like I'm living in a soap opera!

We didn't get out of the Cancer Center until after 5:30 and it took us an hour before we got home. I was to be at church at 6:15 and the boys were going to youth group. When we got home about 6:30, already running 15 minutes late, another friend, Cari Jo, brought over some beef vegetable soup. I was able to get Randy and the boys a late dinner. Thank you, Lord and Cari too!

Randy keeps telling me he can handle the chemo treatments by himself, but I won't let him. I'm smarter than he is. So Donny (nicked named, "Chemosabi") or I have always been with him during treatments. After our day yesterday, Randy was in agreement that he shouldn't try to do this alone. I wasn't going to let him anyway.

We have next week off. Whew! Then we are on schedule at Alta Bates Cancer Center for: 12/20 @ 1:30, 12/27 @ 9:30, 1/3 @ 10:30, a break for a week, 1/17 @ 1:00, 1/24 @ 1:00, 1/31 @1:00. So far the chemo hasn't knocked him down too hard, but last Sunday he felt like he had the flu, so he didn't do much after church. He rests a lot and drinks lots of fluids.

After yesterday, please mark your calendars and pray for us on chemo days. I know this is hard and God won't give us more then we can handle. I am so thankful for friends like you who are there for us. God uses you in such a mighty way to encourage us. We know we're not alone. Look at just yesterday at how many times God used you guys to step in and help me pick up the pieces. Blessings, Randy and Debbie...

Debbie's Thoughts

Around this time, the freezer in our refrigerator got flooded with water, making a mess of everything. I had to get a knife and start chipping away at the ice that had accumulated. I was making slow progress and ended up giving away some of our frozen food lest it go bad. That was about the time our phone rang. It was our Music Pastor, John. He said he had something we needed. I asked him, "Is it a new freezer?" He came over and delivered an envelope with $2,000 in cash inside! The giver or givers didn't want to be known. We just sat down, blown away. Wow! Later that week, another medical bill came arrived, and because of the generosity of those folk, we were able to pay our medical bills. Thank God! I don't think anybody likes debt. I don't know who all the saints were who helped, but God used them in the most powerful way to lift our spirits on a gloomy day. We were truly grateful.

I remember how tired and overwhelmed I was the day Randy passed out at the cancer center and Garrett was forgotten at school and we were stuck in traffic because we were late getting out of chemo. When I got home, I could have just stayed home and taken a hot bath and went to bed. That type of day seemed to become more and more common.

They were long days of getting up early in the morning to get Brady off to the bus at 6:30, then Garrett off to school, and then me to work. Later, I had to meet Randy at the chemo center. The thought of getting dressed, getting the Jr. High kids up and going, doing all the other things necessary in a regular schedule while adding all the problems that come with being a caregiver was often overwhelming. The amount of stress is amazing for caregivers. How does someone go through this that isn't a Christian?

God was so apparent in those days for me. Even though so many things went wrong, someone was in place to pick up the pieces. That particular day is a perfect example. We knew someone at the school who could bring Garrett home, and she was still at the school when I called. Out of the blue, Cari Jo had a crockpot of soup delivered to our house for Randy and the boys to eat. I just heated the soup as I got dressed, and I was able to get the kids to the youth group despite running late. At church, they even served a wonderful Christmas dinner with my favorite tea...black currant! Now how does that happen? Black currant tea? Do you like black currant tea? Do you even know they make black currant tea? I held it together until I saw the tea bag. I knew that God had hand-selected that tea just for me. He was looking after every small detail and letting me know He was there with us in the midst of a very big storm.

That was a grueling day, but God was backing up every play while showing me that even little details don't get left unnoticed.

This was a very important Christmas. For all we knew, it could have been our last one with Randy. We had invited all of Randy's family over for Christmas Eve—his sisters and their families, cousins and their children, his mom and stepdad, and his stepdad's children. Some of the family we hadn't seen in years. We got all the decorations up and the lights were all a glow. Music was playing and the children were laughing because Uncle John was tickling and joking around. We had a wonderful time of visiting and just being together.

One of Garrett's favorite treats is burning the wrapping paper in the fireplace. So he and Randy became "pyros" that day. It's about the only time we used the fireplace. Garrett still makes a big deal about burning Christmas wrapping paper and having fires at Christmas. It warms his heart as he remembers the bond he had with his dad over this. I am sure that Randy is right beside him, looking down from that great cloud of witnesses, enjoying the fire too.

Christmas 2007

Randy & Garrett burning Christmas wrapping paper – "Pyros"

Getting the port implanted in Randy's chest was a very good decision. A port is an access for needles to take out blood and receive medicine without going directly in the arm. We used it so often, and it never got infected. We never had any complications, and as the cancer progressed, it became very helpful. Randy was so reluctant to get it and dug in his feet. I had to convince him this was a good thing. I'm glad I did. It worked so well for him. Randy still passed out when a needle came his way, but his arm wasn't torn apart looking for a vein. I wish we would have gotten it right from the start. It made treatment so easy, and it even made a few procedures and surgeries easier. It saved us a lot of stress and worry. I would recommend it if you are going to get treatments and your doctor thinks it's a good idea.

Important: If you are going to get treatments...I highly recommend checking out a port!

Now that the treatments are over, I can honestly say that we didn't find any benefit when we used the Navelbine and Gemcitabine. That doesn't mean it will not work for someone else.

What we found most effective on Randy's mesothelioma were Alitma combined with Carboplatin. *I truly believe that by going through the Alitma treatments three times, it may have bought us another year.*

Christmas 2007: Brady, Garrett, Randy, Debbie, Colleen & John Kelley

Chapter 7: January 2008 - A New Year

<u>January 1, 2008</u>

Happy New Year! We made it a year! It's been a roller coaster ride. It's the perfect way to describe last year. I am ready to pull the break and stop!

Randy looks super! You wouldn't even know he has cancer. He looks good. I was thinking the other day, is this true? Are the doctors wrong? Look how good he looks! Really, if you saw him, you wouldn't know. He does nap and sleep a lot. He makes it to work and most days, makes it home to sleep. A couple of days a week, he'll make it to the gym for a bit and get some exercise in, then comes home and sleeps.

We have another chemo treatment today. The past three times, Randy's gone without passing out. So, he's doing better with the treatments. The port was the best thing we did. It's been so convenient for blood draws, chemo treatments and other things. We haven't had a bit of worry or infection.

I had several people think Randy was in remission, but this is not the case. Unfortunately, the cancer has been advancing the whole time. A quick recap: the cancer is on the lining "meso" of his heart, diaphragm, and esophagus. The doctors removed the lining of the left lung, and there is a tumor inside the lung, which they didn't remove. The last PET scan shows that the cancer is also in his lymph nodes and there are more tumors inside the lung.

January 30, 2008

Hey Everybody,

Here we are at the end of January 2008. We have our last chemo today with Navelbine. Tomorrow Randy has a PET scan scheduled. We won't get results for a week or so. We really don't know anything new, except Randy is in more pain. He doesn't think the Navelbine is helping. However, the chemo will make him tired and uncomfortable, so the PET scan will give us more info.

As soon as we hear from Dr. Pfister on the PET scan, I'll let you know where we are and the next plan of action. Okay, we are in God's hands. He has brought us this far, and worry is a sin. So I'm not going to worry, but trust in His plan for our lives. Thank you so much for your prayers and we'll get through this.

In Him, Debbie…

February 6, 2008

Yesterday, we met with Dr. Pfister to go over the tests that Randy took last Friday. It seems that there is minimal advancement in the cancer. The tumor has grown about 1/2 of an inch, 6mm, and there is more activity in the lower left lung. The lymph nodes do show some improvement from the November PET scan.

We start a new chemo treatment on Tuesday, 2/12/08. I was hoping for some time off, but we're getting right on it. This is the Alitma, the same treatment we did at the beginning of 2007. He will go once every three weeks, since this is a harder chemo to tolerate. However, it has been shown to slow down the mesothelioma. He did get a bit sick for 4 or 5 days last year, but all in all did very well.

Randy's resting heart rate has been at 105 and higher lately, and we are not sure what's causing that. I think it might be the Navelbine (his last chemo treatment). He had an echocardiogram last Friday, and it showed everything seemed normal. Dr. Pfister has referred him to a cardiologist for follow up.

I was praying for a complete healing and will continue to do so. I hope you will all join me in this. Randy is really trusting God for everything, every little thing. Thank you for partnering up with us in this endeavor. As always, we remain in your prayers and God's hands. Blessings, Debbie...

February 16, 2008

Last Tuesday, on the 12th, we started our third bout of chemo treatments. This one takes most of the day at the cancer center. It went as expected, just a long day. Randy really started to feel bad on Thursday, and came home early on Friday, where he just gets up to eat a bit and back down on a couch somewhere. He does get a bit sick with this; we give him ginger ale, ginger tea, and gin-gin candies to help fight the nausea. I expect this to continue into Monday. But since he's been on chemo treatments for a year, maybe his body might need a bit more time to recover.

He still is in some pain on his left side where the cancer is and in his back. So please pray for relief. The doctor gave him something a bit stronger than Vicadin for pain. We're hoping that this chemo treatment will shrink the tumors some more so the pain will lighten up.

The strain of this cancer has taken a toll on all of us. I'm so very, very tired. I just want to climb in a hole somewhere and pull a seal over me. Just pray that God will give me mental energy. I feel so tired running the boys around; just handling life with "chemo" is a bit much.

Well, here we are, still standing in the need of prayer, and we are in your prayers and God's hands.

In His Love, Debbie…

<u>February 25, 2008</u>

Hi guys,

Just a quick update; this past chemo we had on February 12th was a hard one. Randy was very sick. I was so shocked when he went to work on Friday, because he was so sick on Thursday night, but he made his way there. However, Lana, from KFAX, brought him home early. The next time, I'll make him stay home when he's that bad off. He has lost some weight and we have another chemo on March fourth, so he needs to gain some weight. That's in eight days. They say that people, who keep their weight on during treatments, make it. So he was 191 this morning…he was floating a little over 200, so even if we can pop five pounds on him…

I'm giving him protein drinks, because every time I go on a protein diet, I gain all kinds of weight. Go figure. He is going to the gym today, for a "light" workout. Thank you for your prayers...we faithfully remain in His hands, Debbie…

Debbie's Thoughts

Spirit of Praise, March 10, 2005

"I'm Randy Brady and I want you to listen to the lyrics of this next song. It was taken from the book of Job. Read the book of Job sometime; it can really be inspiring. To see Job's faith and also you learn a lot about stuff and life itself. Apparently, bad things do happen to good people sometimes. And also you'll learn a little about God, that apparently He can be even a little sarcastic sometimes. Read the book of Job, the 38th chapter, in particular. The other thing we learn about God is that He is always there and Job knew his Redeemer lives. Here is Nicole C. Mullen with, 'My Redeemer Lives' on Spirit of Praise, 100.7 The Bridge." – Randy Brady

During Christmas, a dear friend gave Randy a check for $3,000. This lady, June, a single woman, was not rich. I took the gift back to her and told her we just couldn't accept such a generous gift. She said she didn't care what I thought. God told her that we were going to need it and I needed to receive it graciously. So I accepted with the condition that if we didn't need it in three months, I would give it back. She said that she would like to see it paid forward.

At the end of January, when we received our cancer statement, our share of the chemo treatments for the month was $3,078. We didn't have the three thousand, but we had the $78, and my wise friend, who listened to God, had given us the $3,000. Later, I was able to pay this gift and all the other gifts given to us forward and enjoyed doing so. I wonder how these gifts, given to Randy now paid forward, will bless other lives in the years to come. Hopefully, the gifts given in faith will keep on giving and hearts will be changed.

Randy was having some dizzy spells and sweating issues. We finally figured out the heart rate issue. It was one of the pain medications reacting to him. So once we discontinued it, the sweats, shakes, and heartbeat came down.

One of the things we learned from a breast cancer patient was "bone soup." I would get these beef shanks—or you can use turkey and chicken bones—and you boil the bones and make a broth. If you can retrieve any marrow, try and get that out as well. Add some healthy vegetables and meat, then you can make "bone soup." I was surprised how good it tasted. It was like a grandma had made it. Then I thought about how the grandmothers probably did make their own broth instead of buying it from a can. The bone marrow from the cooked bones should act as a building block to help a person make more marrow. It may just be a theory, but it was tasty. The patient, who told us about it, said she strained out the vegetables and just drank the broth. It was all she could keep down when she was nauseated from the chemo.

I told my friend Jan at church about the soup since her husband Frank was also battling cancer. So he and Randy would stand next to each other, complain about "bone soup," and see whose pants were the baggiest. No respect for us soup makers. They are probably up in heaven talking to each other about how good God's banqueting table is and how they don't have to eat "bone soup" anymore.

Randy and I have been working out in a gym called Lakeridge in El Sobrante since 1981. When I walk in the door, I get tons and tons of questions about Randy since so many of our friends there were not on the update list. One friend, Jim, asked to be put on the update list and wanted to help. So he picked up Brady from karate classes. In turn, he forwarded our updates to his wife, Elizabeth, who happened to be a KFAX listener. When she started reading the updates, she realized Randy from Lakeridge was also Randy Brady from KFAX. She was so wonderful. She called, trying to help us with the pain clinics and brought Randy one of his favorite dinners once while I was at the gym working out. While walking around the court with Randy, she discovered that she also knew two of our neighbors. It is such a small world and God is so gracious.

I love Lana from KFAX. Sometimes you'll see me post her Thankful Thursdays on my Face Book page. She worked in the front office and was the second one in the office after Randy. She was my spy. When Randy wasn't looking so good, she would call me. She would come in with breakfast and an extra banana for Randy. If he was sick in the bathroom after a chemo treatment, she would call me, and I'd go get him after he would be off the air. She was like a mother hen to him and cared so deeply. Craig Roberts once told me at a fund raising dinner that Randy is still roaming the halls at KFAX. I said, "Of course he is. He was always so happy to be there." I am so glad he had his time at KJOY, The Bridge, and KFAX. He enjoyed those jobs so much, and it gave him such pleasure to work with some of the most dedicated people in the world.

Chapter 8: March 2008 Allergic to Altima

Actual Internet Updates

March 2, 2008

We headed up on Friday to Redding only to find out the Friday 6:00 prayer meeting at Bethel was cancelled due to a conference. I confirmed it twice before we went up. I wasn't very happy about this.

So we went back this morning at 9:00 for prayer. We were there for about two hours. People were wonderful, praying, and encouraging. There wasn't an instant healing, but maybe healing will come tomorrow or in a week. As Leif says, "You can't put God in a box."

I'm a bit disappointed. I was ready to do the happy dance. Thank you for your prayers. We are exhausted and in need of much sleep. Keep us all in your prayers. Debbie...

March 5, 2008

Just to let you know, Randy's weight was up to 197 yesterday! Yeah!!!

He was up this morning at 4 AM looking really good. I couldn't believe that he had chemo yesterday. I listened to him this morning on 1100 AM, or you can go to KFAX.com, and he sounded super. So things are looking good this day.

The pre-meds they give him with the chemo last until Thursday; that's typically when he starts to feel the effects of the chemo and then for the next four to five days.

March 9, 2008

Hello Everybody,

I wanted to let you all know that this chemo treatment (Alitma) really seems to be helping Randy to breathe and not be in so much pain. So we really think it's making a difference. Our next treatment is April 1st!

We recently took a trip back to Oahu, and Randy hiked up with me to the top of Diamond Head. I don't look so well. I showered with sweat all the way up. It was hot. Randy did better than me. We took some time swimming and just relaxing.

If you all can remember my mother in prayer…she had a stoke two weeks ago, and they found it to be caused by a rare cyst on her adrenal gland. They are continuing running tests. (There is a whole host of other problems that go with it.) She is in Flagstaff, Arizona (far away from her home near Seattle) and will probably be sent to the Mayo Clinic in Scottsdale for help. There have been only 400 reported cases like this ever. So it's rare and serious. Thank you for your prayers and support. Debbie…

April 6, 2008

Randy is really doing wonderful. He was down this weekend with his nausea pills, ginger ale, and "ball games." When he had his chemo treatment last Tuesday, he had an allergic reaction to the carboplatin. The one that really helps is the Alitma. However, they work together. He can still take Alitma, but we are not sure if it will be helpful.

We are also having a situation with my mom. I was in Flagstaff, AZ, this week at the medical center with her. They were taking good care of her, but couldn't help the underlining problem. Her stroke was caused by a tumor on her adrenal gland. This rare tumor has wreaked havoc on her body, attacking her kidneys, heart, blood pressure, and blood sugars. She is making her way to the Mayo Clinic in Scottsdale to hopefully find a specialist in endocrinology. The Mayo Clinic has seven, and five of them are surgeons. Please pray they find a surgeon who will help us and that she is strong enough candidate for surgery.

Thank you for all your prayers. We know it works. Randy is doing so well. Yes, he hiked to the top of Diamond Head in Hawaii just two weeks ago! Where would we be without your prayers? I don't even want to know. We are blessed because you care. Blessings, Debbie...

Debbie's Thoughts

Having friends who are truly our brothers and sisters in Christ is such a blessing. So many times we needed help, and our friends were there to help us. Leif came and stayed with the boys while we were in Redding at Bethel Church. He is like a big teddy bear, and I'm sure the boys had a good time with him. His wife Heidi and he had two boys of their own at the time. They now have a little girl. We had hands laid on Randy for healing and spent the weekend with our friends, the Hitly's, in Redding. Jennifer also battles with her own cancer and is a real trooper. I love the way she keeps fighting, a true soldier in the midst of a cancer war.

During part of this time, I was in Flagstaff, AZ, with my mother, who had a major stroke. This happened when Randy had an allergic reaction to a chemo treatment. I felt so bad I wasn't there with Randy while he struggled through the reaction. I was so torn and wasn't sure if my mom was going to pull through her medical issues. Her heart and kidneys had also been damaged as a result of the doctors treating the stroke and they couldn't stabilize her blood pressure well. Add to that Randy's chemo treatments, and I was completely torn between where to be.

Ron Kennedy was with Randy, however, and helped the nurses get the allergy medications and tubing right. Randy and Ron talked about it like it was a big event. I am sure it was with these two clowns. What can I say about Ron Kennedy? Our family just loved that man. He and Randy were such good friends and worked together in the children's ministry at church. My boys loved him so much; he was like Sponge Bob to them. We really relied on Ron a lot to help us through some really dark days. Thank you, Ron! You were such a blessing and a true friend.

When I left Flagstaff, I wasn't sure that I would see my mom here on earth again. It was so difficult to walk away and leave her in God's hands and just pray. So much I had to leave in God's hands. She was in such a critical state. In the five days I was with her, nothing had changed. My brother Chris was on his way and would take over my duties with her. That gave me some comfort to know that she and my step dad wouldn't be alone in Flagstaff. The doctors still didn't have her blood pressure stabilized and couldn't transport her to the Mayo Clinic in Scottsdale until they did. My stepdad was so weary and tired. Finally, the doctors found a cyst on her adrenal gland—apparently it was a very rare problem. The TV show House had an episode with this medical condition on it. Mom did pull through and lived almost another three years. She was able to come home to Washington, walk again with a cane, and lived a quiet life with lots of doctor appointments.

Are you in a pit of despair? Are you so tired and finding no rest for your soul? There is only one that can come in and fill you from the inside out. It is the God that made you, formed you in your mother's womb. It's Jesus. He loves you and won't leave you to handle this alone. On the darkest of nights, He is there. Even in the bright lights of the hospital, He is there. You will never have to be alone through any of this. Even though there will be times you think you are. When you look back, you will realize He was carrying you through the deepest of valleys. Just pray a simple prayer and ask Jesus to come into your heart and He will never, never, leave you; it's a promise He made. He has heard your cries in the night and loved you even before you were born.

Go ahead! Reach out for Him today. He knocks at the door; all you have to do is let Him in.

"Lord, I'm lost and weary. I feel so alone. I need You in my life. Please forgive me of my sins, and Jesus, come into my heart and make me whole. Thank you, Amen."

It's that easy. Welcome to eternal life. It begins today.

Chapter 9: May 2008 Holding His Own

Internet Update

<u>May 19, 2008</u>

Hello everybody!

Wow, six weeks since the last update. It's so hard to believe. Randy is holding his own. Since he is only getting 1/2 of the chemo treatment (since he had the allergic reaction to one), he isn't as sick from the treatments and we are at the cancer center for less time. We are hopefully going to get a PET scan before the next treatment on June third. If you see Randy, he looks super. He does get tired, but overall, doing well. This is truly remarkable how well he is doing. I just give praise to God for hearing our prayers.

My mom is home (near Seattle), seeing her own doctors and she is happier. They put in a port for dialysis (she was close to kidney failure). She named her port "Bubbles" after Ella Fitzgerald. Ella Fitzgerald was a remarkable woman jazz singer who overcame some major obstacles with an unbreakable will. After they put the port in, my mom's numbers went up, so they will test her every three weeks. She still needs to see other specialists before we can get her totally well. Her attitude is one of a fighter, and she is also doing okay for now, but not out of the woods yet. Thank you for your concerns, thoughts and prayers!

Okay, we are as always, in your prayers and God's hands. Blessings, Debbie...

June 6, 2008

Hello everybody,

It's been 17 months! Can you believe this journey? It's been incredible to see God's hand on us, the blessings you all have been to us. Your prayers have been heard! If you were to see Randy in the store or anywhere, he looks amazing. Nobody would have a clue that he's sick. He is still working, still working out, still playing ball with Garrett, doing super, just super, actually, remarkable.

We had some good news yesterday. It looks like the Altima is doing a super job. There has been a decrease in the cancer! ;) From our PET scan at the end of Jan and from our PET scan at the end of May, the tumors have gotten smaller and the lymph nodes don't show signs of cancer in them anymore! I wish we had news that it was gone or we don't have to have more treatments, but we don't. I think now we know for sure the Altima is working, and it encourages us to keep the treatments going.

We are also looking into a second mode of attack, boosting the immune system. We already use nutrition for anti-oxidants, but now we are going to be checking out probiotics and vitamins for boosting his immune system to fight the cancer off as well. There are also some blood tests that can check for deficiencies.

Wow, it was a super day yesterday. For the first time, I felt like dancing at the cancer center. Usually, I'm running for the door.

Thank you so much for the prayers, encouragement, support and love. It helps us pick up the pieces every day and move on. We love you all. As always, we are in your prayers and God's hands.

Randy & Debbie…

Debbie's Thoughts

During Spring Break, my brother Dave and his wife Michelle and their two twin boys came down and had a week of rollercoaster madness—Marine World, Great America, Santa Cruz. They also went to Carmel and Monterey. I was so thankful that they took our boys with them. Randy couldn't really get around, and we had a treatment scheduled on their week off. Besides, I knew he couldn't be left alone or be able

106

to go on rollercoaster rides. So my family came and grabbed the boys and off they went. What a time they had. I'm sure they left their mark on every ride in every park. It's kind of funny to see my twin nephews with their cowlicks and green eyes looking so much like Brady, but still resembling their mom too. Then there is Garrett, totally different, who has dark skin, eyes so black you can't find the pupils, and black hair. But then I have a niece, Sara from my brother Rick, who looks like Garrett. It is such fun to see how the family resemblance spreads across even to cousins. It was a screaming good time for all.

My mom was still recovering from her stroke in Arizona. We had flown her home on one of my frequent flier tickets and she stayed with one of my brothers. My stepdad drove the RV home with one of his brothers.

My mom struggled to accept her situation. I remember her meeting with the neurologist, and after he had the audacity to recommend physical therapy, my mom told him what he could do with his "physical therapy." I asked her an important question, "Do you want to walk again?"

She said, "Of course."

I said, "You call that doctor up, say sorry, and take that physical therapy as fast as you can." She didn't realize that stroke patients recover faster with physical therapy. They now have physical therapy on the same floor as stroke patients and in some cases, start therapy the same day. I had just listened to Chuck Swindoll on KFAX talking about his stroke and the whole ordeal he went through. Thanks to him, I knew how important physical therapy was and was able to relay that information back to my mother. She had my stepdad call and setup the appointments. She worked really hard and came back almost 100%.

Randy enjoyed this summer of just hanging out with the boys. He liked throwing the ball in the court with Garrett. He watched a ton of reruns of Frazier with the family. We bought a Jack Russell and named him "Eddie." This dog will stare at us, just like the dog does on Frazier. We also bought the DVD's for Cheer's. Randy liked to laugh a lot. He would walk to Starbucks, in Hercules, on Saturday and meet Darby, Alan, and Jerry for coffee. He would try and get to Lakeridge a few days a week and keep an exercise schedule on non-chemo weeks. He would usually fall asleep watching television.

Speaking of Darby, he is a really good friend. I remember after the surgery where the doctors removed the lining of Randy's lung. Randy came home and wanted me to go to Starbucks and get Darby. He had bonded with Darby and wanted him to know what had happened to him. So I went down to Starbucks at the appointed time, and there was Darby in line for coffee. So, I tapped him on the shoulder and asked that after he got his coffee would he mind coming home with me. He said he didn't need coffee and told me to lead the way. Darby had been in a few motorcycle accidents and Randy had prayed for his recovery. Darby had healed real well. I want you guys to know this was the only time I ever picked up a man and brought him home.

These were such trying times for me and I would often ask, "Why are we here? What is our purpose?" I often wondered and pondered, "What is God's will?" One day, I was reading my Bible and these versus struck me hard. I realized this is why we are here—not only for His good pleasure—but to help one another. Think of Zion as your neighborhood, city, town, or even a person.

The Spirit of the Lord GOD is upon me, Because the LORD has anointed me To bring good news to the afflicted; He has sent me to bind up the brokenhearted, To proclaim liberty to captives and freedom to prisoners; [2] To proclaim the favorable year of the LORD And the day of vengeance of our God; To comfort all who mourn, [3] To grant those who mourn in Zion, Giving them a garland instead of ashes, The oil of gladness instead of mourning, The mantle of praise instead of a spirit of fainting. So they will be called oaks of righteousness, the planting of the LORD, that He may be glorified. – Isaiah 61:1-3

In the past few years, I've seen so many broken hearted people that have been discarded by society and the church. It's truly sad. Instead of being given flowers, they are literally left with the ashes of their loved one. Do you know someone who had someone close pass away? Can you lift them up? Do you have some good news you can share? I believe "the prisoners" are those who are in some kind of bondage or addiction and not necessarily just those in actual prison. I know a big God that can help people overcome all addictions. Somehow we need to become a "caring" society, reaching out to our neighbors and friends when they have a tragic loss of a loved one, house, health or job and are suffering. Yes, it will take some of your time, and yes, you might have to miss a meeting or have to tape a favorite show. Trust me when I say they are worth it. One day it will be you in a boat without a paddle, and God says you are defiantly worth it.

For God so loved the world (you) He sent His only begotten son, so that none would perish but have ever lasting life. – John 3:16

I am currently attending a church on Wednesday nights that is "broken friendly." I have to drive over a bridge and fifteen miles one way to get there. They have a grief share class, which I am attending, a divorce care class, which my friend is attending, and a Celebrate Recovery, which people attend, but you can't say who is attending. It is a safe church because you don't have to pretend everything is okay and fine. You can be hurting and be real with your emotions. We all have seasons of grief and pain. One of the worst things you can do is to stuff those feelings down and bury them. They come back later to haunt you. They then are called "triggers" and PTSD.

You are the person in their life that can make a difference for them. So be that person, step up and be a hero.

The meetings brought out something interesting to me, something that has reoccurred several times after Randy's death. Sometimes after a loved one dies, the family just pulls away. It surprises me how often I heard this story in different forms.

While waiting at the cancer center one afternoon, Randy and I met a lady and her two children. Two years earlier, her husband had died of lung cancer during a simple procedure that had gone awry—and that she had authorized.

His family chose to blame her, wanting nothing to do with her or her children. This was so devastating to her and her children, because it was like a whole family had died. Now she is suffering from breast cancer, and only her two young children were there to be of any comfort.

After hearing that story, Randy would call and talk to his family in person or by phone before each treatment or procedure. He wanted to assure them that he was in control of his faculties and his decisions for procedures. He knew the risks and had done his research and then shared them with his family to give them as much peace as possible.

So open those lines of communication and talk to your family. I think this was a super thing that Randy did for his mom and sisters. He made them a part of his decision making process, and they could ask questions and knew ahead of time what was happening. There were no surprises.

Similar stories of the woman at the cancer center, repeats itself over and over in grief classes and in our church, where the spouse's family pulls away after the death of the family member. The reasons are all different, but the results are the same—devastation. One lady shared how her husband had died due to some medication complications after a knee surgery went bad. Her husband's family was so upset with her, blaming her instead of the doctor who had prescribed the combination of medicines. By the time she called 911, he was gone. She never thought his family would blame her for his death, but they did. Another friend of mine, from high school, passed away from complications due to diabetes. Her husband

and son won't communicate with her family…reasons unknown.

It breaks my heart to hear these stories. If you and your loved one are going through something like Randy and I were, you may want to discuss details with your family. There is so much pain and suffering in these circumstances that we become walking wounded. When family pulls away from someone who is left behind, it just adds to the pain and suffering. It's not only the loss of a loved one, but a whole family.

I heard years ago that when a parent dies, it's common for the child or children to wish it was the other parent who had died. They will express so much anger and hate towards the surviving parent and idolize the parent who passed. The child or children have to work through their grief. Kids don't have the coping skills of adults and don't have life resources to draw from, so it's a real rocky road. Our pediatrician said the boys could be in their thirties before they could really begin to process the death of their dad. I understand this and often have told them they would have these feelings towards me and it was okay. I didn't want them to feel bad for having them.

If you feel you need it, try and find a support group. As you go through treatments, it helps to know you have others in your boat. You can find resources and ways to cope. You don't have to make a long term commitment. Sometimes just a couple of meetings can help you get over a hump.

Chapter 10: August and September 2008

Pain and Petco Park, San Diego

<u>August 20, 2008</u>

Hi guys,

It's been a while, and we have been enjoying our summer. We have continued the chemo treatments and have been in a treatment plan since last November consistently.

We had a CT scan last week and it showed some small tumors around Randy's heart, but the surgeon who took out Randy's lung lining saw cancer around the heart when he did the surgery, so it isn't new news. Dr. Pfister has ordered a PET scan to see if that would give us more information. However, you know how insurance companies work; ***we have to wait for approval***. I'll let you know if anything significant shows up.

At this time, we are going to continue with treatments, even though I am tired! As long as Randy is tolerating things well, we are just going to stay on the same plan. I thank you for your continued prayers.

Here is a picture of Randy on the 4th of July with Ron Kennedy on the left (our children's minister) and Buster Donohue on the right—good old long time buddy from First Baptist.

Blessings, Debbie...

August 22, 2008

A difference two days can make! Randy woke up yesterday in horrible pain. We spent nine hours in emergency yesterday, trying to make him comfortable. We weren't too successful in this endeavor.

Today, we got in to see Dr. Pfister, and man oh man, the drugs we are going to get. I'm on my way to the pharmacy right now, and I think they might think I'm a drug dealer, but we have to get a handle on the pain and then can wean him down.

Apparently, a tumor is pressing on a nerve causing the muscles to cramp. So, we will schedule radiation with Dr. Swift. We will follow up with Dr. Pfister on Tues and check his pain level.

We have a trip planned for Labor Day weekend for him to go to San Diego with the boys to see a ball game in the new PETCO Park. I already got the tickets. So I hope we get this all settled so they can go on the trip. I'll update you guys in the middle of next week. Well, as always, we are in your prayers and in God's hands...keep praying for him. Blessings, Debbie...

August 23, 2008

Okay...we got the pain under control, now we will wean Randy down slowly. He's a bit loopy. Thank you for the prayers...Debbie...

September 3, 2008

Hi guys,

A few weeks ago, I sent an update saying how much pain Randy was in, and we are now controlling it with medication. At this time, he is fairly comfortable.

Randy went last weekend to San Diego with his friend Buster (who drove) to PETCO Park. Randy wanted to see the new stadium in all its glory! He took Brady & Garrett, and passing through Los Angeles, they picked up Mark Leopold & Kyle Donohue. They all had a fabulous time. I heard a lot of gas was passed. Happy I stayed home and missed the flatulent air waves!

We saw Dr. Swift today at the Alta Bates Cancer Center, and he went over Randy's last CT scan and was able to see the tumor in Randy's lung and felt that he can radiate the bottom half of Randy's left lung. This should be able to release the cause of pain, (tumor pressing on a nerve). There are other tumors in his chest, but not causing any problems. So there is no need to radiate them and cause any needless tissue damage.

We will continue chemo to help keep those other tumors to a minimum. He will lose half the function of the left lung. Lung tissue is permanently damaged with radiation, but hopefully, we then can wean him off the medication and he'll be able to move without difficulty.

He will continue chemo treatments. We feel that it has bought us 13 months of Randy working and doing well. He has a chemo treatment tomorrow. However, we will take a break from chemo while doing radiation. We go in for a PET scan Monday, 9/8, and then Dr. Swift will work out a schedule to start radiation treatments. We will meet with him 9/10 to get more details after Dr. Swift has a chance to view the PET scan.

116

I just wanted to keep you in the loop. Thank you for your concerns and prayers. We know we are loved. Blessings, Debbie…

September 9, 2008

Hi everyone. Here is an update on what's up.

Randy is still in some pain. I've taken away driving privileges until we can wean down the pain medication. I drove him to Fremont yesterday @ 4 a.m., and we tried to get him on BART this morning (up at 3:45 a.m.). But after three times back and forth to the BART station, he was just too sick to make it. The doctor thinks possibly his "episodes" these past few mornings are due to a conflict in medication, so we are going to try and alternate doses tomorrow and see if that might help, and maybe I'll drive him into work Friday and we will try the BART thing again next week.

We met with the radiologist and the good news is that Dr. Swift really thinks he can help Randy get out of this pain. It may take five weeks or so to do it, but we go back to the cancer center tomorrow. They will do a CT scan, and then put the info with the PET scan we did on Monday, then add the physics, and then take 4 to 5 days to organize the radiation doses, and then he will begin radiation treatments every day. Also, if the BART thing works out, he can go to the Ashby BART station and a shuttle will take him to the cancer center. I'll be able to get Garrett from school. Then hustle to Berkeley to get Randy.

Please keep us in prayer. It's been a rough few days. I'll update again when we get radiation treatments going.

Blessings, Debbie...

September 22, 2008

Hi guys, latest update:

We went to radiation oncology today and Randy starts radiation treatments on Wednesday 9/24. It is about 1/2 hour every day, Monday through Friday. The times are mostly at 2 PM, 3 PM and a couple of 4 PM for the next six weeks. He will continue to get treatments at the Alta Bates Cancer Center on Dwight in Berkeley. He will leave work in Fremont and take BART to Ashby. Then take the hospital shuttle to the cancer center, where I or a friend will meet him to bring him home.

For the past few weeks, Ron Kennedy and I have been driving Randy to KFAX studios in Fremont at 4:20 a.m. We just can't let him drive on that much pain medication. I am recruiting help; if anybody would like to take a morning run, let me know. I am usually home about 6:10 a.m. We are hoping in three or four more weeks, we can start weaning him off of the pain medication and he'll be able to get his keys back. Also, just pray for Randy, he has lost some weight; it may be the chemo, cancer or the pain meds or all three. I'd like to see him gain at least 10 lbs back during this radiation treatment. That will be only a God thing!

What do we need? I'll need Garrett picked up from Pinole Middle School 2:30, M – Thursday, & 1:30 on Fridays. (I'm asking Nikki to do that for me) to free me to be with Randy during radiation.

I am so grateful there is a way to help Randy get out of this pain. Dr. Swift is very confident this is going to work. We also have a pain management doctor, Carol Jessop, MD. She is wonderful, attentive, knows how to treat nerve pain and, more importantly, has a prescription pad!

Thank you for your prayers, dinners, help, support, cards, calls, e-mails, and encouragement. If you have a free afternoon to meet Randy in Berkeley or would like to take an early morning run to Fremont, please give us a call.

Blessings...Debbie…

<u>September 28, 2008</u>

Okay guys, here we go again. We have an extra consideration on the table: Women of Faith, Friday Night. So I am looking for someone to be here with Randy until Brady gets home. Buster, will you please Randy sit? Below is the ride confirmation for the upcoming week. If something comes up and you can't make the morning run, just call, and I can drive him down.

Also, remember, Randy's on radiation treatments. He won't tell you if he's not well. So, if he looks sick, acts sick, doesn't look right, please bring him home, even if he tells you that he is okay. Otherwise he will go to work and be sick. We need him to come home and rest. There is backup at the radio station, so don't worry if you have to bring him home. You have full discretion. I give you the power to bring him home or call me, and I'll come and get him.

If he needs immediate medical attention, call 911 and have him transported to Alta Bates Emergency. They have all his records and PET scans on file.

<u>I have for morning KFAX rides @ 4:20 a.m. Pick up:</u>

Monday: Robert, Tuesday: Chris, Wed: Terry, Thurs: Jay, Friday: Manny

Radiation Pick Ups:

Monday & Wednesday: Debbie, Tues: Handsome Joel & Beautiful Janet

Thurs & Friday: Donny

Garrett Pinole Middle School Pick Ups:

Monday - Thurs: Nikki, Friday (1:30 minimum day) Ron

Brady: (Friday Night):

Bring home after ball game: Krista/Matt

Randy watch (Friday Night):

Until Brady gets home: Buster

The last words my Grandfather Freed spoke to me were, "Thanks, I couldn't have done it without you." I echo those same words back to you. All of you are a blessing to us and thank God for each of you. Blessings, Debbie...

Debbie's Thoughts

One of Randy's favorite experiences with KFAX was Fellowship Days. He loved baseball and loved watching the games. He couldn't believe all the perks that came with being on the air. I think if he had the opportunity to broadcast a game live, it would have been a dream comes true. He enjoyed it so much that we had to plan our vacations around Fellowship Days. When Donny Moore came out at the A's game with the muscle men tearing up telephone books and rolling up the frying pans, Randy was in his element. He loved it. He would join the guys by taking his little two inch business card and tearing it in half. What a hoot! One year, Randy left vacation two days early so he could make the Giant's Fellowship Day. On another occasion, Dave Dravecky came to one of the Fellowship Days. Randy introduced himself and spoke to Dave for some time about cancer and faith. Dave Dravecky was a major baseball player with the San Diego Padres and the San Francico Giants. He had his own battle with cancer which caused his arm to be amputated. Dave knew, what we all are learning, our identity is not in cancer, but in Christ. He now is a featured guest speaker at many events. Dave later led a word of prayer for Randy at the AT&T Stadium in San Francisco. What a blessing that was! It spoke volumes to all of our hearts.

We had the best 4th of July Celebration that year. So many friends came out for a BBQ and to watch fireworks. The house and yard was packed! It was a time of fun and lots of laughter. I'm so glad we had friends over and enjoyed each other while Randy was with us. We had the BBQ going, lots of salad and desserts. Everybody brought their kids. Some went on top of the roof to get a better view of the fireworks and some walked down to the bay. I remember our insurance man wasn't too happy about people enjoying the rooftop scene. It makes me smile to remember that fun day. I'm glad we had it and so many of you came.

July 4, 2008
Ron Kennedy, Randy & Buster Donohue

In August, things really changed. As Randy's pain went into hyper mode, our lives took another change. We were so dependent on so many people. I had to ask for so much help. I needed help getting Garrett home from school, Randy to work, and to Bay Area Rapid Transit (BART). I needed to get Randy from KFAX to BART. From BART in Berkeley, he could grab the shuttle to the cancer center or I could pick him up—if I got a ride for Garrett. Because of all the medication he was on, I had to take away his car keys. We had to figure out all these transportation issues without him being able to drive.

We never got the pain under control. From this point on, Randy's pain never got below the level of four. We continually tried to chase the pain down and illuminate it. But it seemed like we could never get on top it. I was constantly on the phone with Blue Cross or pharmacies. I would wait at the pharmacies having panic feelings...like Dustin Hoffman did in the movie, "Rain Man." I would watch the clock and think, "Oh my gosh, in twenty minutes Randy's pain is going to be unbearable!" While waiting for the pharmacist to try and find a way to get the insurance company to authorize the medications, I thought I was going to throw up.

I believe it was around this time that Randy's thinking started to change. He started looking towards heaven and leaving earth as a way to escape the pain. He bought a book about heaven written by Randy Alcorn, wanting to know about the place that we are all dying to get to. I believe Randy somehow was partly transcended. He had one foot in heaven and the other on earth. Perhaps God was meeting him down here to help him through this terrible ordeal of suffering.

Regardless, His focus became clearer in making every day count. He wanted every day he had left here on earth to make a difference "a hundred years from now." He started thinking in those terms. If it didn't make a difference a hundred years from now, he didn't bother with it. He also didn't want to be left alone, and we started getting creative with "Randy sitting."

Every time I left the house, he wanted to know when I was coming back. He never really cared before. But now he was anxious. If something went wrong, he wanted me with him. I kept my cell phone with me, which is something I hate to do. He would often go with me, if the boys were not home.

We had built our lives on solid rock and we prayed and clung to our faith. We knew God had a big plan for our lives. We knew that Randy's days were numbered before he was born. We knew that God orchestrated our lives, our friends, our church, our doctors, and our treatments, all before we ever came into existence. God met us coming and going and this was the time that tested our faith.

Jesus taught us that we would have tribulation in this world—not that we might have it, but that we will have it! Expect it. But be of good cheer for He has overcome the world. We had tribulation (cancer), not because we didn't have enough faith, or that we did something wrong, or because God was picking on us, but because we live on a cursed earth. This could have happened to anyone. However, we received Jesus as Lord and Savior, and we have assurance that, for believers, life continues in a different way, called eternal life.

If you confess with your mouth Jesus as Lord and believe in your heart that God raised Him from the dead you shall be saved. For with the heart man believes resulting in righteousness and with the mouth he confesses resulting in salvation. – Romans 10: 9-10

"I have told you these things, so that in me you may have peace. In this world you will have trouble. But take heart! I have overcome the world." – John 16:33

I am so grateful that Randy had this time with his softball friends and our boys at PETCO Park in San Diego. They had a ton of fun and Randy really loved hanging with his buddies. It will be a fond memory for my boys.

Petco Park, San Diego, September 2008: Mark Leopold, Buster Donohue, Kyle Donohue, Garrett, Randy & Brady.

Randy had trouble getting to the BART train. He had dizzy spells, and his heart would race, causing him to sweat profusely. He was not coping well at all. Looking back, we never did get a clear answer on why this was happening to him. His cardio checkups all worked out fine. I think these may have been panic attacks.

I started getting panic attacks a bit later after he did, then I had them daily after he died. It was only recently that I was able to connect the dots. They say that hind sight is 20/20.

I guess so, but some things you can't understand until you live it—and even then, it may not make any sense until much later. Even four years after Randy's passing, it still doesn't make sense.

Randy never did get his car keys back. I just couldn't let him drive with that amount of narcotics in him. He didn't understand and would complain to his doctors. I remember Dr. Swift asking me, "Why would you take away Randy's keys?"

I couldn't believe he asked that question. It should have been the doctors taking away those keys. So, I told him, "It's a lot of medication, and if Randy got into an accident, it wouldn't matter whose fault it was, he would be blamed." Only a half of one of the fifty pills he was taking would have knocked me out for eight hours. There is no way Randy should be allowed to drive. Honestly, if you could see his pain chart, he was hurting enough to knock out four horses! Sometimes he would say the oddest things. The doctors at UCSF Pain Management would come out and meet him because they couldn't believe he could still walk with that much pain medication in him.

Despite the difficulties, things worked out great. Randy loved the morning ride time with the guys. It was one of his special times. He would often tell me how much he looked forward to it. He would pray for each person picking him up and for their time together. It was wonderful to have so many friends stepping up to drive and give him rides. I would get calls, emails, or verbal requests at church from guys who wanted to give him rides. Nobody arranged it, but I believe God orchestrated it. I only drove a few times a month after this because most of the days were taken. These rides went on for eleven months, a true gift of love. What we thought was going to take a few weeks, turned into almost a year. So many men and a few women came and gave him rides. As I said before, over two hundred people came to our rescue. It was truly amazing and gifts of grace.

It was also an opportunity for Randy to spend time with Brady. Brady got his driver's permit and needed a seasoned driver to go with him. It made Randy feel special. He got to spend time with Brady and Brady learned how to drive. They would talk about Mustangs, not the horse, but the cars. They also were able to have bonding time and when Randy wanted to run an errand and I was busy, he had a driver.

So many people asked to help, giving me their numbers. I would say, "I'll call," and I did. There were times I would pick up this list and ask for help. I felt very humbled asking for help because I was always so strong and independent. I am woman and I can roar. I can bring home bacon and fry it up in the pan. I hated how dependent on others this cancer made me, how broken I had become. It had flattened me to the floor. I didn't recognize myself. I had panic attacks, couldn't sleep, felt frustrated, helpless, and oh so very desperate to find a cure for cancer. I had to rely on God and others to get us through this terrible time. But by asking for help, we could keep Randy working on KFAX and it gave him a purpose for living. It was such a ministry to us and others.

So many people came and helped us. How does that happen? Not because we are good people, not because we are cute and beautiful—well, I'm cute and Randy was funny—not because we are super rich—which we weren't—and not because we are really friendly. It happened because these were Christian people who loved the Lord and wanted to make a difference in the world and help someone who were in need. We didn't deserve this outpouring of goodness and love. This is called, GRACE! People did it out of the goodness of their hearts and because of who Jesus was in their lives! Jesus was the reason why so many people came to our rescue and I am forever grateful to the Lord. So this story is a testimony of the difference The Lord can make in the community. Thank you, to each of you.

Chapter 11: Pain Management

Debbie's Thoughts

I wanted to take a chapter to talk about pain. It was terrible, and I won't sugar coat it. I don't want to scare anybody, but it's best to be prepared for this and make plans and not need them. We heard that Mesothelioma was painful, but we had no clue what to expect and how to treat this. We chased our tails for a year. We never got ahead of this pain. Knowing that Randy is now out of this kind of pain is the only thing that really comforts me about his death—besides knowing he is with the Lord.

Okay Meso Patients! This is where the rubber meets the road. I say plan for the worst, but expect the best.

You must have a pain management plan before the pain hits.

We didn't know where to go or what to do when this pain hit. The emergency room is regulated, and there is only so much pain medication they can give. It wasn't near enough. Dr. Pfister quadrupled the amount of pain medication and double timed it, giving us *eight times the amount of pain medication that was the maximum amount allowed to be given in the emergency room.* So having a pain specialist on hand or knowing that your oncologist will understand the type of pain that can be associated with mesothelioma is very important. If your oncologist isn't ready to work with you to set something up ahead of time, find someone else. It is that important. Don't live with regrets, prepare.

Important: For meso patients, have a pain management plan before you need it! Emergency Rooms won't be able to handle this kind of pain.

We loved Dr. Carol Jessop. She is a pain specialist in Oakland. However, she had so many patients and so little time. Maybe things are different now, and she might be worth a visit if you are in the area. I wish we could have cloned five or six of her. She was very patient and caring and really understood pain. She was the one who introduced us to methadone and kept increasing the dose. She even taught Dr. Pfister about pain management.

But it was very difficult to catch Dr. Jessop for prescriptions. Because of the amount of narcotics Randy was taking, he needed to be monitored. We needed to see her once a month. However, she was very busy, making it difficult to get an appointment to see her. There were a few times that we would have completely run out of pain meds if it wasn't for Dr. Pfister being available at the cancer center. I would give him a call and drive over to Berkeley, then to the pharmacy. A backup plan for pain is imperative! Dr. Jessop's information is in the back of this book.

If you find a doctor isn't available, and it's too hard to get in, find someone else. We ended up going to UCSF Pain Management Clinic in San Francisco. Getting Randy his pain medication prescriptions were easier there. We didn't have to panic, down to the minute, every month that Randy was going to run out. I couldn't function in that kind of a panic state every time some pain medication began to run out.

Once it took me a week to chase down a good prescription for Randy. I was literally at the counter with only twenty minutes left before Randy was going to be in horrific pain. It was so stressful waiting for the pharmacy to try and get the insurance company to sign off on it. It was truly a nightmare. You must be proactive on the pain management. It was a full time job.

This problem with the insurance company only underscores our problem. We had a private plan with Blue Cross. They had a pharmaceutical watch dog that authorized the meds. They were not allowing Randy any more morphine, which was odd. Apparently, they thought he had enough. When I called, they put me on hold for over an hour. Finally I got someone on the line. They didn't care that he was a stage four cancer patient. I yelled, "That's ridiculous! I am going to call the police. That was malice."

"Go ahead," she said, "I'm in the Philippines."

Wow! I said, "Does Arnold Schwarzenegger know about you? You are not in America, not an American, and you are denying my dying husband his pain medication?"

I was so angry. I literally didn't know what to do. We ended up changing the dose and that, for some reason, went through and we were able to get more morphine. I did file paperwork against Blue Cross with the State of California in the Health Insurance Department. There is an emergency department that you can fax your complaint to and they will respond within 48 hours or sooner if you are denied treatment. There probably is one in every state. However, since Randy was on a private company plan, they couldn't help us. Good thing I learned about changing the doses.

I know I said this earlier, but some insurance companies get kick backs from manufacturers. So if you try different brands, they may go through. Or if you switch the dose, from 10 mgs to 20 mgs, then you can cut the pill in half—if <u>it is not a time released tablet</u>. The doctor must see the patient monthly while writing the script, so get your appointments in advance.

Randy had to take pain meds around the clock every two hours. It was important not to give some of them close together, so I put together a spread sheet. Then we got big pill boxes. I used a purple highlighter for night and yellow for day. At one point, Randy would mix everything up, so we wouldn't let him get his own pills.

Time	Pain Med	Pain Med	Pain Med
1:00 AM	2 Norco	40 mg Oxycotin	3 30mg IR Morphine
3:00 AM	2 Norco	40 mg Oxycotin	6 30mg IR Morphine
5:00 AM	1 Norco	3 80 mg Oxycodne	2 200 mg S R Morphine
5:30 AM	8 10 mg Methadone	3 300 mg Nurontin	
7:00 AM	1 Norco	40 mg Oxycotin	3 30mg IR Morphine
9:00 AM	2 Norco	40 mg Oxycotin	6 30mg IR Morphine
11:00 AM	1 Norco	3 80 mg Oxycodne	2 200 mg S R Morphine
1:00 PM	1 Norco	40 mg Oxycotin	3 30mg IR Morphine
1:30 PM	8 10 mg Methadone	3 300 mg Nurontin	100 mg Topamax
3:00 PM	2 Norco	40 mg Oxycotin	6 30mg IR Morphine
5:00 PM	1 Norco	3 80 mg Oxycodne	2 200 mg S R Morphine
7:00 PM	2 Norco	40 mg Oxycotin	6 30mg IR Morphine
9:00 PM	2 Norco	40 mg Oxycotin	6 30mg IR Morphine
9:30 PM	8 10 mg Methadone	3 300 mg Nurontin	100 mg Topamax
11:00 PM	1 Norco	3 80 mg Oxycodne	2 200 mg S R Morphine
3 days	Fentanyl Transdermal 250 mg.		

Randy's Pain Meds 7/2009

Randy's Meds 8/16/2009

	BREAK TRHOUGH PAIN		
7:00 AM	400 mg Methadone	400 mg Morph SR	
9:00 AM	2 Norco	6 30 mg I R Morphine	240 mg oxycotin
11:00 AM	2 Norco	400 mg Morph SR	
1:00 PM	3 80 mg Oxycotin	1 Norco	900 mg Nurontin
	BREAK THROUGH PAIN		
3:00 PM	400 mg Methadone	2 200 mg Morph Sr	
5:00 PM	2 Norco	6 30 mg IR Morphine	3 80 Oxycotin
7:00 PM	2 Norco	6 30 mg IR Morphine	
9:00 PM	240 mg Oxycotin	1 Norco	900 mg Nurontin
	BREAK THROUGH PAIN		
11:00 PM	400 mg Methadone	Ativan	2 - 200 mg SR Morphine
1:00 AM	2 Norco	6 30mg Ir Morphine	3 80 mg Oxycotin
3:00 AM	2 Norco		2 200mg SR Morphine
5:00 AM	240 mg Oxycotin		900 mg Nurontin
			200 mg Topamax
	300 mcr Fentynol patch		

135

Chapter 12: October and November 2008

Radiation and Disneyland

Actual Internet Updates

<u>October 17, 2008</u>

I've gotten some calls and e-mails. Sorry guys, I've not been in my regular spot for a few weeks (the gym). So I better get an update out.

First of all, thanks to all the early morning drivers who have graced us with their presence to deliver Randy to KFAX. It's truly been a blessing to him to have your company. He loves his "manly" time.

Randy is in his 17th day of radiation and the fatigue is starting to wear him down. He has also battles with nausea every day. (Unlike other radiation treatments, this encompasses the esophagus and stomach.) We have another 12 treatments on the schedule. Dr. Swift explained that with each treatment, Randy will continue to get more and more fatigued. Also the radiation treatment results are delayed, and it may be sometime before Randy is out of pain and we will see the benefits of the treatments. So we are looking at the end of November before we can see Randy starting to "perk" back up.

I have asked Randy to consider possibly taking one day a week off work (Wednesdays), so he can have that time to rest and heal. I'm only asking for 3 days; he's thinking about it.

We have made plans to go to Disneyland after the last radiation treatment and before chemo treatments resume. We will just go down for a few days. Brady now has his driving permit, so it will be an exciting trip! Randy can rest in the van—all the seats recline. I booked a hotel across the street, so when he is tired, he can go and rest, and the boys can stay in the park. If need be, we can put him in a wheel chair. (I'm not sure he will let us.)

Thank you for your encouragement, love and prayers. We remain in His grace, Debbie...

October 28, 2008

Wow! We were surprised today!!! We were told we were going to have six weeks of radiation and our schedule had us going until November 5th, but today, the technician told Randy that ***tomorrow is his last day***. We couldn't believe it, so we double checked, and yes, tomorrow is his last day for radiation.

I'm not sure how long of a break we get before going back to chemo, but I'm hoping for a few weeks. He is really tired, lost some weight, and has a burn on his back, which we are treating with aloe gel. Now we wait and see if it will work to get him out of pain. The radiation has a residual effect, and it can take about three weeks before we know the benefits.

Dr. Swift said that Randy may not be able to drive until the end of November, if the treatment works. *It has to work!! We need it to work!!* So please keep that in prayer. The radiation treatments will release the tumor on the nerve. We are taking the "if" and rebuking it!

We are taking the boys to Disneyland. Brady and I will be doing the driving down and back. Randy will be sitting back and relaxing, snoring and telling corny jokes to try and impress us with his witty humor. Of course we will just roll our eyes, like old times.

Thank you for your prayers and encouragement. I am so humbled to have been graced by your love for us. It's amazing that this all started twenty-three months ago. Thank you for meeting us where we are.

In His Grace, Debbie...

November 3, 2008

Once again, you are coming to our rescue. We appreciate the early morning rides to

Fremont. Randy seems to be over "the throwing up" stage. I think the radiation had a part in his sickness. However, he is still in pain. We have to wait until the end of November to see if the radiation helped. Blessings, Debbie...

November 18, 2008

Well, it's been almost three weeks since the last update. We are still praying, fighting, and doing everything we can to stay happy and well.

We went to Disneyland last weekend, and Randy was able to hang out in the park from 10 to about 4:30. We got him an electric wheel chair, and we were able to get through some of the lines quickly. We met my cousins, and Brady took off with Kyle Donohue, and everybody had a good day.

Randy wasn't up to a second day in the park, so we watched the Dark Knight from the hotel, the boys went bowling with Randy for a couple of games, and then we met Mark Leopold and family for dinner at Downtown Disney. We drove home the next day.

Brady drove a few hours going down on Hwy 5 and coming home. He did a good job, and Randy sat in the passenger seat to give him instructions.

So far the radiation treatments have not deterred the pain. We have about another week to give the radiation time to work. We are going to see Dr. Jessop, pain management, on Wednesday and work up a new plan.

We meet with Dr. Pfister (oncologist) on Tuesday to discuss the chemo treatments. Randy did get a clean bill of health from the cardiologist. The tumors are not affecting anything that is cardio related.

Attached is a photo of us at Disneyland. I'll let you know what chemo treatments are in store. But if I don't get back to you before Thanksgiving, please let us wish you the best of Thanksgivings and know that we are thankful for the gift of you! Blessings, Debbie...

Disneyland: Debbie, Garrett, Randy & Brady

<u>November 20, 2008</u>

Hi everybody,

Here we are from the last two doctor visits, this week. Dr. Pfister wants Randy to rest and gain some weight, take another PET scan, and then decide in three weeks or so how he looks and if we will start another chemo program.

We saw Dr. Jessop today (pain management doctor), and she is increasing medication for pain and giving him something for anxiety. She will be on call for any needs that Randy might have. Randy is still not driving.

So we are going to have a wonderful Thanksgiving. I am hoping we don't start chemo until after Christmas!!! I am going to "relish" the break.

Once again, we are always in your prayers and God's hands, Debbie…

Debbie's Thoughts

Randy never did take a day off from work, despite my urgings. He always wanted to be at KFAX—sick or not. He had a plastic bag in his jacket that he could use when he needed to throw up. He would go, and then I would get a call that he was down the hall in the bathroom. I would drive to Fremont and pick him up. However, it was always after his shift on the air. If you would have listened to his broadcasts, you wouldn't have known he was sick. He'd get right back on the air with a smile in his voice.

I also want to take this time to brag on the KFAX staff. They were so wonderful and supportive. If Randy needed extra time for treatments, they worked it in. Someone from the office would give Randy rides to the BART station every day and I would meet him on the other end after I would bring Garrett home from school. Lana, the receptionist, would bring him a banana every day. She was the one who promised to call if he wasn't feeling well. I knew the guys there were always looking out for him. Amy would get him a room at a local hotel for some of the night events. His good pal, Andy, who lived in Tracy, drove all the way to Pinole to drive Randy to Fremont one morning. I'm sure it was close to a hundred miles. Randy truly felt a part of the team and knew he was well loved.

We have a DVD that the staff of KFAX made as a tribute to Randy. His coworkers and guest speakers on KFAX each said a few kind words to him and about him. I am so glad that he had his dream job on the air and that Craig Roberts had hired him to come on KJOY back in 2001. It was one of the most exciting things that could have happened to Randy. Thank you, KFAX. Randy loved you all so very much. He'll be waiting next to Jesus to welcome all of you home.

Disneyland was both a good time and a bad time. I know the boys wanted to spend so much more time there, but Randy could only handle about eight hours in a chair. He was tired and I was tired too. The next day he told the boys he couldn't do it, but maybe bowling would work. The boys went with it, but I knew they were disappointed. I could have gone back in the park with the boys, but I had a migraine and didn't feel like I could leave Randy all alone in a hotel as he had been so sick since the radiation treatments.

Randy got to see the Muppet Show at Disneyland that first day. He loved the Muppets. We have Muppets all over our house and every movie they ever made. It was wonderful to sit next to him and watch his face light up as Kermit the Frog came out on the ladder in 3D. Randy sat out on a lot of the rides, and we did a lot of waiting for the boys. My cousins, Ray and Mary, joined us, and it was fabulous to watch their small kids' faces light up as the magic of Disney captured their imaginations.

Good trip or not, Randy was still in pain. We had such high hopes for the radiation. However, Randy's pain didn't diminish with treatment. Nor did we see a decrease in the cancer. I'm not sure of the benefits. His voice changed and his breath became short after each treatment. He did have a burn on his back, which we slathered aloe cream. I would cringe and cry when I would rub it on. It was so tender and all the hair was gone. If we had to do it over, I don't know if we would do it. Did it somehow slow down the growth and number of tumors? Nope. I can't really say that it did. After a radiation treatment, he was always nauseous and had a hard time keeping food down. However, he was also taking a lot of pain medications which, no doubt didn't do him much good either. Unlike the Alitma treatments, where we defiantly could see the tumors were smaller on the PET scan, the radiation didn't seem to do much.

From here on out, Randy's pain was always getting away from us. We were on such a time sensitive schedule that we had to administer pain medication throughout the night. Add to that the difficulties getting the medication approved through the insurance company and it was very difficult. He really was over all the state limits on his pain medications, so there were walls we had to break through. Finally, I filed an emergency request through the state's health department. I faxed a request on Randy's behalf, and they were supposed to respond in 48 hours. I was able to work with the pharmacy to get this done before the request was handled.

So if getting pain medication becomes complicated, see what help you can find from your state's health department. **Another trick is to change the dose. Sometimes that can put a prescription through. Instead of 40mgs, see if you can get 20mgs and take two or change the brand name. Some insurance companies get benefits from pharmaceutical companies, and one brand will go through where another brand will have a hard time.**

Chapter 13: December 2008

Christmas in Washington

<u>December 1, 2008</u>

It really does take a village to keep Randy going, and I am so grateful for each of you. I know that I could take him in to work every morning, but it was taking such a toll, and I am so thankful each morning you come to the door. If something comes up, if you get sick, or if your car doesn't work, I'll be the backup; please give us a call.

Just so you know, Randy still gets sick from time to time and has increased his pain medication. If there ever is a situation, please call 911 and have him taken to Alta Bates Hospital. They have all his records in the computer.

On Friday, I am whisking Randy away to San Diego for the weekend as an early Christmas gift. We have an ocean front room on the beach (great deal) at the La Jolla Shores Hotel. We're leaving boys at home.

If you spot any conflicts, please let me know. We are looking forward to ocean waves and setting sunsets. Once again, thank you all so very much. Blessings, Debbie...

December 4, 2008

I wanted to share with you where we are with Randy's treatments. Randy saw Dr. Swift on Tuesday, and he told Randy he was the *longest living mesothelioma patient that he has seen at Alta Bates, and by far, the one with the best quality of life.* December 8th will mark the two years point when we started this whole ordeal.

We are investigating a clinical trial at UC Davis just for mesothelioma patients. It is pharmaceutical funded, so we don't have to involve insurance. We are not sure of all the side effects and what kind of appointments the trial would entail. We are getting more information sent to his doctor. I'll let you know if we decide to try that route.

The most amazing thing is that with the help of his many friends, Randy is still able to make it to work. If you don't know, there is a different person at our door, *dark and early*, at 4:20 a.m. to drive Randy to Fremont, so he can work at the KFAX. That is 45 miles one way!

Then someone from work drives him to the BART Station. I then meet Randy either at the cancer center or BART Del Norte and bring him home. I think it's an important part of his health to keep on being productive. Thanks to all of you.

Brady & Garrett continue to do well, going to school and karate classes. Brady is a Jr. black belt and Garrett is a yellow belt. They love it. Both boys exhibit exceptional art talent, not just mom talking. Brady's artwork is often featured on the school's website and he has gotten awards for his exhibits. We are encouraging Brady to get an art degree. So far, we are planning on him getting his AA at DVC and then on to the Art Institute in San Francisco for a BFA. Garrett's artwork is also very good, and it seems like both boys inherited my brother's talent.

I am still working part time and taking care of Randy, doctor appointments, and all the paper work for insurance and lawyers...keeps me on my toes. Thank you all for your prayers and best wishes. We wouldn't be here without you. Blessings, Debbie...

December 18, 2008 (Bad News, New Hope)

This is a hard one to write. We got the results of the PET scan that Randy took on Monday, Dec 15, today. It seems the cancer has grown. Some of the tumors have doubled in size and the report says, "Innumerable nodules in the left chest." There has been a slight decrease in size of nodules in the area where he had radiation. But you know we have seen these nodules decrease last year, so it can happen again!

Randy is still in quite a deal of pain. We saw Dr. Jessop on Wednesday; she is going to refer us to another pain specialist (hopefully we will see next week) to either freeze the nerve or give him some kind of pain pump. If he is given the nerve block, maybe we can decrease the amount of pain medication and he can drive again!

The new hope, a clinical trial (AZD 2171) at UC Davis, is showing some success. Randy, so far, qualifies for the treatment. Paper work has been sent, and we did get a call from UC Davis saying they did get paper work and will be calling to set up an interview. What I have read about this trial is that it's a pill, taken for 28 days, and then lab work is needed throughout the process. The side effects are minimal. I don't know what this requires on our part, how often we will need to go to UC Davis, how often he will need lab work, and do we have to go to UC Davis to have the lab work done. I bet we do; they'll have to have complete control of the trial. When this happens, I need more help with the boys, pickups from school, rides to karate, and just plain "hanging around fun time." You know...maybe Randy will be the one who breaks through this cancer! Maybe! He will be the one that will beat it. I'll keep you all updated as I know more.

We are so lucky to be celebrating another Christmas with Randy, to have him here, still able to go to work (thanks to all his good buddies). Every day is a gift. God has blessed us with so much; we are grateful every day.

Keep us in prayer. I believe it's the only reason Randy is still with us. God still has a purpose for him. We remain in your prayers and God's hands. Debbie...

December 22, 2008

Okay, I have a situation until I have exhausted all avenues. You know me, a dog with a bone. Randy does know. Randy doesn't qualify for the clinical trial at UC Davis due to the fact that he was on two chemo treatments at Alta Bates. Only one chemo is allowed to follow the protocol of the trial. I have made

149

numerous calls to oncologists and Randy's lawyer, Steve Kazan's office, this morning for assistance in getting him considered somehow.

Our best bet, besides God sending us a miracle, is that Randy be considered "off protocol" as a compassion case. I've sent in the request at UC Davis and it's under consideration. This trial is the only thing we have been able to research that has made an impact on mesothelioma.

Please keep this in prayer...that Randy would be considered for an "off protocol" program. Actually, we were thinking this might be better. Because in the clinical trial, only 50% of the patients gets the medication. This way, we will know he is actually taking the AZD 2171.

Thank you for the prayer. I've been praying all morning, trying to remain in His Spirit and not be upset. I thought I'd like to pull you each in for prayer as well. Debbie...

Debbie's Thoughts

I made some time to get away with Randy. We used to fly away to San Diego every few years for my birthday. I loved the beach and to watch the ocean sunsets. A friend told us about La Jolla, so I booked a room and made plans. When we got there, we were exhausted. I love the smell of ocean air and to hear the seagulls. Randy was tired and I ended up with a migraine. We did venture out for dinner, but made it an early night.

The next day, we took a walk on the beach. I still had a headache, but Randy was looking about. He kept saying, "This is the place! This is the place!" I didn't know what he was talking about. He told me we had stopped at this spot some thirty years before with a choir tour on our way home from Mexico. It all came back in a flash. I had been driving a van and kept running over the barriers. Bev, in the back of the van, would complain and yell, "Ouch!" I have photos of me and my friends on that beach. I was skinny then.

I said, "What do you mean this is the place?"

He said, "We walked on this beach and we talked. I then thought you might be the one for me."

I didn't know that, because it was about a year before we started dating. I thought it was super that we had come full circle and now stood in the same spot where he had fallen in love with me all those years ago. It is wonderful to have heard that and to realize his love for me. It is a precious memory.

At this point in Randy's treatment, I felt especially helpless. We had exhausted all our chemo and radiation options, and since our doctors didn't have anybody hang on this long with mesothelioma, we were breaking new ground. It was such a desperate point that we all felt like we were just grasping at straws. When we were turned down from the clinical trial, I really was scared. I didn't have a plan to look

151

forward to. This is where I wish I had known about Dr. Johanna Budwig and her protocol. I know Randy would have gone for this as it made so much sense and it was such a healthy alternative. This is where I kick myself all the time for not knowing about this. We did juice, ate yogurt, and Randy ate flaxseed in his cereal. But I didn't know about sulfur protein. Somehow I have to quit kicking myself and let others who are fighting with cancer know about it.

This Christmas was Randy's last with us. We flew up to Seattle to spend Christmas with my family. It had snowed, and that was an ordeal, especially me swirling around in the cul-de-sac with the rental car. What can I say? You've heard me write about growing up with four brothers. Well, I love my four brothers. We were like an army growing up in Hawaii. If you are in trouble, they'll come running and swinging some bats. One of my brothers came out and told me to let up on the gas, so I did. I just kept swirling the car. Another brother came out and said, "What are you doing? Gun it!" I just got out and let them pull it out of the snow. Then I parked down the hill from the cul-de-sac where there was little snow.

My boys stayed at my brother Dave's house, so they could play with their cousins, and Randy and I stayed at a hotel. Randy wasn't doing well, so he spent a lot of time resting. Randy did get very sick on Christmas morning, and I was glad we were in the hotel. After the radiation treatments, Randy couldn't keep much food down, but in the hotel, we could stay quiet while he went through his sickness and wouldn't feel bad about making a mess.

We went over to my brother's that afternoon when the rest of the family showed up. My mom was also there. She was still weak and tired after her stroke and the damage to her kidneys and heart. We gathered around the tree and the kids all opened their gifts. There were so much family with all the aunts, uncles and cousins there. Then we played board games, puzzles and video games. Mom and Randy were napping and quietly visiting with each other. Everybody was so kind and tender towards mom and Randy. The kitchen was open over the counter. We all could visit with one another while cooking. It was our last Christmas to have our family together. I have wonderful photos. I didn't realize how much our family dynamics would be forever changed.

Christmas in Seattle 2008

Top row: Randy, Paul Freed, Chris Hubbell, Dave Freed, Rick Freed, Chuck Hubbell.
Bottom: Debbie, Monica Freed, Tonia Hubbell, Michelle Freed, Elizabeth Hubbell

Chapter 14: February 2009,

New Pain Clinic and New Chemo

Actual Internet Updates

<u>February 2, 2009</u>

Just to keep everybody in the loop. Randy had his second chemo treatment this past Tuesday 2/3 and is now starting to feel nauseated. He still plans on going to work on Friday, taking Monday off to spend with Brady. It seems like the effects of the Gemcitabine are fairly minimal so far. We'll see what the weekend brings.

We went back to UCSF pain clinic today and they redid the epidural. It won't be until Saturday through next Thursday before we know if the epidural worked. We go back in two weeks, if needed, to take the next steps.

We now have to see a pain specialist for pain medication every time Randy needs a refill. FDA regulated, so tomorrow, Randy is taking BART from work. I'm picking up Garrett at 1:30 from school, and we will meet at the doctor's office in Oakland tomorrow at 2:00. We have to work out a better system in getting

Randy his medication and not be chasing down prescriptions and pharmacies that have the medication on hand.

If you say a prayer, please pray that the epidural will take effect and Randy can lie down again. He's been sleeping sitting up since November.

Thank you for teaming up with us. The rides, dinners, encouragement, cards, errands and prayers have meant so much to us. Sometimes, just the littlest things can mean so much. You all are God's hands and feet, reaching and carrying us through this ordeal. Blessings, Debbie...

February 26, 2009

We finished the last chemo in the session last Tuesday and asked for a new schedule. Dr. Pfister wants to wait until we get another PET scan. Randy has a tumor on the outside of his ribs. We noticed it last November and it was small. However, recently it "looks" and feels bigger. Dr. Pfister said he isn't sure if it's because Randy has lost weight that it looks bigger or if the tumors are growing. But since most of them are inside the chest, we will get a PET scan next week.

Randy is still in pain, but we think the epidural has given him a little relief. He does seem to get some "attacks" in the ribs. We are hoping the PET scan will show us more.

I was reflecting yesterday about the past two years. It's been a journey, but I started thinking about all the help we have received, so I started writing down names. Over 140 people have helped us pick up kids, drive Randy to work and to BART, brought over meals, sent us help for medical bills, taken Randy to appointments, chemo treatments, ordered us dinners, and picked up medication for me, Brady and Randy, especially when my migraines were real bad. I must say, when the going gets tough, **God sends in His best.** So from the bottom of our hearts, thank you for the help, the prayers, the pickups and dinners. I make sure that the boys see the kindness we are given—that they know, in the hard times, God does show up. We will always be grateful for your imprint in our lives. Blessings, Debbie...

Debbie's Thoughts

We didn't get the compassion consideration for the clinical trial at UC Davis. With the help of Kazan's Law Firm, we were able to get in and see Dr. Jahan at UCSF. He recommended a chemo treatment called Gemcitabine. So we had a plan. I always like to have a plan.

Dr. Jahan also referred us to UCSF Outpatient Pain Management Clinic and we met Dr. George Pasvankas. Dr. Pasvankas took Randy's case to heart, showing great interest. When we came to the clinic, doctors came out of their office to meet Randy. They were just amazed that Randy was still with us, that he could walk and work while being on so much pain medication, and that he could comprehend everything that was being discussed. If you take a look at Randy's pain charts, you will understand. It is truly jaw dropping.

I loved the staff at the UCSF pain clinic. They were so tender and compassionate with Randy. Every time I called with a problem, they returned the call right away. You'll see as we move on in the book some of the invasive procedures performed to try and control Randy's pain. Truly, they turned over every stone to help us control Randy's pain. Both Dr. Pasvankas and Jahan's contact information are at the end of this book.

Randy never did lie down to sleep again. We rigged our bed with a board and propped pillows so he could get comfortable sitting up. So his head wouldn't flop over, we took a neck cushion and put the opening towards the back of his head. This way his neck wouldn't be all stiff in the morning. He would read his Bible at night until he fell asleep. He said that if he didn't fall asleep reading God's Word, he would think about everything that was going on and get scared. God's Word was a source of comfort for him in his darkest hours. It

157

gave him courage and anchored him in what was sustaining him through the pain.

He also never slept more than a few hours without having to take more pain medication. I don't know how he functioned. For every day he had left, he wanted to do good things, to make a difference in someone's life. If he went to work and got a child sponsored for World Vision, he made a difference. If he could call a listener who was struggling with cancer, he made a difference. If he could share how God was sustaining him through his cancer treatments and make a difference in someone's life, then that was a good day. He also continued to go to the fellowship games and concerts and introduce the guest speakers or players. He was so happy to do that. He had cancer, but cancer didn't have him.

Amazingly, especially to me, Randy never complained. He sometimes would tell me something hurt or that he had tightness, but he never yelled, got mad, or got upset. He was always grateful for the help I would give him and thanked me almost every day.

He once visited a friend who was in a care home because of too many strokes. He told me it was so sad. This friend's wife put him in that home, divorced him, and just left him there. This really upset Randy. I think he was worried that his situation would be too much for me to handle, and I'd put him in the home with his friend. I would never do that as long as it was in my ability to prevent it. He was always grateful for anything done for him. I never saw Randy angry or bitter during the whole of his illness.

God often puts angels in our path, and I hope you notice some on your trails. For us, one such angel was a dear friend named Jeri. She just happened to be a chemo nurse. She and her husband came over for dinner one night, and while eating on our deck, the subject of Randy's mouth sores—a result of the chemo treatments—came up. Randy had mentioned these sores to Dr. Pfister on a number of occasions, hoping something could be done, but they had so far gone untreated. Jeri shared information about a 'magic' mouthwash. There is a mouthwash that has an active agent in it that will numb the sores, kill fungus, and has an antibiotic in it. So that was just a wonderful gift. We called and spoke to Megan, the Physician Assistant at the cancer center about it, and she called it in. Worked like a champ.

My loving and caring family from Washington, New York, and Connecticut got together and ordered dinners for us. They lived in different parts of the country and weren't available to offer practical help, so they used a company to deliver prepared dinners that went in the freezer. All I had to do was warm them up. This really came in handy when we would come back late from UCSF in San Francisco, and all I had to do was get something in the oven and add vegetables. It was a big help. So if you are far away from your loved one and wonder how you can help, this was a great idea. You could also send a gift card to a local restaurant they could stop at on the way home from treatments.

I want to say that we couldn't have done this on our own. God was always there to meet us and help put us in the right place at the right time. When we turned a corner and found the path ahead to be so dark and bleak, God had

159

someone there to guide us and help us. It was truly amazing how really and truly *you* are His hands and feet. We are still so humbled and grateful and feel so undeserving. We needed so much help and we got it. So much of the time, I just felt like the walking wounded. It was like I was in a war zone that left me shell shocked. But everywhere we needed it, God had a first aid station along the way.

There came a time I didn't recognize myself; I was broken. I now know I had to rely on God's strength. I did not have this kind of power, not for 32 months. I had become worn and tired, and I needed strength greater than my own. I was always the strong and determined one, and now I was having panic attacks and not sleeping well. I didn't take well to antidepressants as my stomach didn't tolerate it. I also couldn't think clearly taking the medication so instead, I would use breathing techniques and lots of prayer.

I made a deliberate decision not to drink. I thought if I did drink, I would never stop. With my dad and mom also sick, every time the phone rang, I'd have to hold my breath. Every day we just had to keep trusting God. As the years go by, I kept thinking I had to keep holding on to God. But now I realize, like He did for Peter as he was sinking in the sea, that it was Jesus who reached down and held on to me! I will not drown in this sea of despair and anxiety. He will lift me up! And set me on solid ground. He will give sound mind and purpose. And He will hold you up too if you are sinking. Just call on His name and He is right there. No other name I know has such power.

But seeing the wind, he became frightened, and beginning to sink, he cried out, "Lord, save me!"

Immediately Jesus stretched out His hand and took hold of him, and said to him, "You of little faith, why did you doubt?" – Matthew 14:30-31

My soul clings to you; your right hand upholds me. – Psalm 63:8

I am a different person now. You cannot go through so much loss, hurt and rejection and not be changed. My priorities are different. I am stronger, wiser, have greater discernment, and gained a compassion for those who are ill. I have an understanding for those who are caregivers and a new view for children who have ill parents. I have a deeper appreciation for nurses and doctors. I see life with a different set of eyes, a set of eyes that have seen cancer rip apart a family and change lives forever. I am not the person I was or will ever be again. Am I better? In some ways, but today, I recognize that I am still broken and humbled and still in the need of continued healing. I know where to go, and I will continue to move forward to the high calling.

I'm not saying that I have this all together, that I have it made. But I am well on my way, reaching out for Christ, who has so wondrously reached out for me. Friends, don't get me wrong: By no means do I count myself an expert in all of this, but I've got my eye on the goal, where God is beckoning us onward—to Jesus. I'm off and running and I'm not turning back. – Philippians 3: 12-14 (MSG)

Let us run with endurance the race that is set before us looking unto Jesus, the author and finisher of our faith. – Hebrews 12 1-2

Chapter 15: March 2009, Appendicitis Again

Actual Internet Updates

March 8, 2009

Yesterday we had a situation or as Randy likes to say, "an issue." Randy went in for his PET scan at 8 a.m. Everything went well, left a bit after ten. We tried to get refills for his pain medications, but Dr. Jessop's office was closed. Since Randy fasted, we went to breakfast, then did a bit of grocery shopping, got back home about 12:30. When we checked our messages, one was from Dr. Pfister saying the PET scan from that morning **shows an acute appendicitis**. He said to get Randy to Alta Bates Emergency as soon as possible, and we did.

After the ER doctor took some tests and spoke to the radiologist who read the PET scan taken by Dr. Pfister, they decided **not to take Randy into surgery**! Randy has no symptoms of appendicitis except what is showing in the PET scan. It's 13 centimeters and inflamed. Due to the chemo, radiation, and cancer, he isn't a good candidate for surgery. There is a possibility that the enlarged appendix is a side effect of the chemo treatment. They want to wait it out. So we are keeping track of his temperature; so far the highest is 96.8. He has no abdominal pain, whatsoever and no vomiting. If any of these things changes, we need to get him back into the ER.

I did share with the ER doc that we had a son, who did not have typical signs and went around with a ruptured appendix for five days. But Garrett did complain of some abdominal discomfort, but not as much pain as he should have had. If Randy does show any other signs, they will do the surgery.

I am still not too sure what to think of all this. I just couldn't believe it. It's almost like a joke.

I would have been happier if they did the surgery, got the appendix out, so we would not have this hanging over our heads. So here we are with a ticking time bomb, and I just can't figure this whole thing out. I've decided not to worry about it. It doesn't help.

I'm not in control; God is. I can't do the surgery, but God can make it happen. We have known from the beginning that God has been with us, and He will continue to lead the way. We get the rest of the results of the PET scan on Tuesday. I'll give you an update again then. Blessings, Debbie...

March 12, 2009

I've decided to get a second opinion. Dr. Pfister gave me the name of a surgeon in his office building. We had a 2 PM appointment.

We met with the surgeon for the second opinion. He is in agreement with the doctors at Alta Bates. It's an incidental finding and Randy doesn't have any of the typical symptoms, and he wouldn't do surgery, and we can go ahead and fly to Hawaii for our anniversary trip.

I, once again, shared our experience from Garrett's ruptured appendix. He didn't think I remembered things quite right. When we left, I was still quite apprehensive. We will keep an eye on Randy's temperature and see what happens.

March 28, 2009

Well, Aloha!!

We thought we'd sneak off to Hawaii and have a few days to ourselves before starting the next round of chemo. *Well the surprise was on us!* After the assurance of two surgeons at home that the PET scan appendicitis was an *"incidental finding"* and Randy was not in any danger, they encouraged us not to cancel our trip, so we went.

We were there for only one day when Randy developed a fever and some pain. So after some arguing—Randy wanted to go to the Cheesecake Factory for dinner and I wanted him checked in at the hospital—we prayed. We asked God to lead Dr. Pfister in telling us what to do. So when we called him, he said go to the hospital and get a white count. The count was slightly up!

When we handed the Emergency Room doctor a copy of the PET scan, showing appendicitis, he was stunned. I can still see the look on his face when I handed him the report. So they did a CAT scan, admitted him, and gave him IV antibiotics. After three days, he decided to take the appendix. The surgeon at Straub Hospital thought the chemo would have an impact on the white blood count and that's why it wasn't elevated. The surgery went so well. They did it laparoscopically; the doctors were not deterred by his cancer treatments. Randy was in and out in less than two hours. The staff and surgeon at Straub Hospital in Honolulu were fabulous. They were confident and took such good care of Randy. They released him Saturday and cleared him for flying yesterday and we got home last night. When the surgeon met us for a follow up, she said that pathology found mesothelioma in the appendix. This is why the PET scan lit up. We were lucky to get that out before the appendix burst. Whew! We won't forget this trip.

We were visited by the Honolulu Police Chaplain Andy Kikuta (also pastor for Alliance Church) who prayed with us, drove me back to the hotel, gave us an Aloha goodbye with a ride to the airport and took us by the Honolulu Salem Communications (Radio station from Randy's work) who also prayed with us. I met a new friend in the waiting room and we were busy watching time fly by while sharing life stories.

I want to personally thank each and every one of you who came to the rescue and took the boys to and from school, doctor appointments, driver's test, church, brought over food, medications, and just loved on the boys while we were gone. It was like the cavalry to the rescue!

We have just decided to take some time off of treatments for a month or two and let Randy heal and rest up from this whole ordeal. We will continue to meet with Dr. Pfister for checkups, but no chemo for a while.

We are in such good hands. Thank you for everything that you have given us and have done for us. You have blessed us in so many ways. In appreciation, Debbie...

Debbie's Thoughts

The day after the PET scan that showed the "appendicitis" we had a "guy's day" in our house. I left to hang out with a girlfriend and the guys just came whenever they wanted to. They played cards, watched games, played a little basketball, and the younger guys played video games. I had made a huge crockpot of pulled pork and the wives made salads. It was a great day for Randy, appendix scare and all! We were so lucky to be surrounded by so much love. Thanks guys for making this a special day for Randy.

But the appendix scare became much more. We took Randy in to get it checked out, but the doctors dismissed the idea. This was disconcerting since two years earlier, Garrett, our youngest son, woke up one Monday morning with a pain on his right lower abdomen and no one thought it was appendicitis except me. In fact, my first thought had been of appendicitis. I called a nurse in my Bible study group and she said to check Garrett's temperature. It was a little above normal, but I was concerned and kept him home. During the course of the week, I had taken him to the doctor three times, and they ran a ton of tests only to determine that it was probably just a virus. I still had my reservations and told Randy that if Garrett wakes up in terrible pain, we were going to the emergency room immediately—which is exactly what happened.

I told the emergency room doctor that I thought it was appendicitis, since his temperature had now reached 99.6. We had an argument about it. She ran more tests and then sent us off to the University of California San Francisco Medical Center with a "mass." Long story short, it was not a mass, but a ruptured appendix. The doctors at UCSF felt it had ruptured the first Monday I had taken him in to have it checked out.

For the next two weeks, Garrett and I practically lived at UCSF, but God had sent us through a series of mazes and ended up with the World Famous Surgeon, Dr. Michael Harrison, to help Garrett. Dr. Harrison has a wing named after him at UCSF and he is the father of fetal surgery. It was his finger on the cover of Newsweek with an embryo's hand reaching for him. God had placed us in the best hands in Heaven and on Earth to help Garrett. We felt very fortunate to bring Garrett home, 13 pounds lighter, but alive.

Despite the entire trauma we had gone through when Garrett's appendix had ruptured, the doctors still insisted that I remembered the story wrong. This amazed me. Garrett didn't have a fever, he wasn't in terrible pain, until after surgery, and his white count was only slightly elevated, and the thing still ruptured. How can a mom remember something like that wrong? With Randy now having the same issues with his appendix, I was like Dustin Hoffman in "Rain Man" one more time. Could Randy handle a ruptured appendix? I couldn't sleep. I was on pins and needles. I wanted to throw up. Here we go once again…another ER has turned us away. We didn't know it, but God had another plan lined up called Straub Hospital.

Straub Hospital in Honolulu was amazing. From the moment we walked into the ER until we were wheeled out, we were treated with kindness and compassion. Those doctors looked at the PET scan report and went into action. They stood in amazement that Randy was even allowed to come to Hawaii. I remember the look on the ER doctor's face when I handed him the PET scan report that said he had appendicitis.

The surgeon at Straub was incredible. She looked at the whole picture as a "cancer patient with appendicitis." The reason why he wasn't having pain, she decided, was because of the amount of pain medication he was taking. It could mask some of the pain. His lower white blood count was probably due to his "chemo treatments" and his bone marrow wasn't making the white cells. So coming to Hawaii for our anniversary was probably God's hand on us. It wasn't much of a fun trip, but one that probably bought us another five months of being together as a family. If that appendix went, especially with the cancer in it, he may have only had days. Really, it was such a relief to get that ticking time bomb out.

The last time I was on Oahu, I took a trip to Straub Hospital. Dr. Kwan and the whole staff that was there to take care of Randy has now moved on. They were all there at the right time and place to take care of us. I realize, just like Garrett ending up at UCSF instead of Children's Hospital in Oakland, that God had a better plan for Randy: Straub Hospital in Honolulu. God put it all in play.

"For I know the plans I have for you," declares the Lord, "plans to prosper you and not to harm you, plans to give you hope and a future." – Jeremiah 29:10-12

Chapter 16: May and June 2008 Pain Pumps

<u>May 1, 2009</u>

Hi everybody,

This last epidural, 3/12/09, did not give Randy the relief it has in the past. He has been in horrible pain for the past six days. I was able to get him into the pain clinic yesterday, and they have adjusted his medications for now. It may take a few days to see if it works.

We also found a compounding pharmacy in San Francisco, across the street at UCSF Hospital (different location then pain clinic and cancer center), and they did a fabulous job getting everything set up for Randy. I have to send them a thank you note.

Dr. Pasvankas is recommending the Spinal Cord Stimulator. It's a battery attached to some electrodes that will go to Randy's back. It gives out a signal with impulses and keeps the brain busy, like talking to someone on the phone. When the tumors press on the nerves, and want to send a signal that there is pain, it won't go through. There will be a busy signal instead. It's a bionical piece, so now we can call him the Bionical Man!! Once it is working and operational, we can then wean him off pain meds. We are waiting for insurance approval and will move forward with or without it if the trail is successful.

Randy is still working in spite of the pain, and I just want to thank all of you who are helping us out. We appreciate the rides, the doctor appointments, the dinners and prayers. I truly don't know where we would be without all of you.

I'll keep you updated. Thank you for blessing us. Debbie...

June 4, 2009

Just a quick note. I know a lot of you are calling and e-mailing. We go back to UCSF tomorrow to just have the epidural checked out, look for signs of infections, change the dressing, and things like that. I won't let them take the pump out. It seems to be providing some relief. So we will have to take this temporary situation and make it permanent, which will mean surgery.

We just increased the dose on the pump Tuesday, and Randy seems to get less, breakthrough pain. In addition, he still is taking large amounts of pain killers by mouth. Randy is still making it to work, with pump in hand. I went in with him dark and early Tuesday, and his medication ran out while he was on the air at 8:30; we knew ahead of time that would happen. So he makes a joke and I change out the bag and loaded him back up. He had me "wave to everybody so they could see me." It's radio!

So it's been a hard week, but we are making it though. Thank you all for your concern, best wishes, prayers and all the help. Blessings, Debbie…

June 18, 2009

Hello everybody,

We were excited to celebrate Brady's graduation!! Yippee!!! When Randy was diagnosed, we were told Randy wouldn't be here for this event, but Praise God, He was. We have a few more milestones ahead: Randy's 54th birthday 6/27, our anniversary (24 years) 6/29, and Brady's 18th Birthday, July 16th. We would love it if Randy was here for those dates and so much more.

The epidural pump UCSF put in at the end of May isn't working as well as we hoped. At this time, he's taking more pain pills than before the pump was installed. So we have to remove the pump and find a different plan. The doctors at UCSF are recommending and intrathecal pump. This would go deep into the spine, a catheter would be threaded up from his lumbar region to the thoracic area, and then medication would go in deep through the spinal column. This means a 4 to 5 day stay in the hospital while they monitor his heart, breathing, and blood pressure, plus get the right amount of pain medication. If this is successful, he will require much less pain medication, and he could remain mobile so he can still make it into the radio station.

We go in on Thursday (June 18) @ 2 PM for the intratheical pump. So I expect to have Randy home, maybe Monday or Tuesday the following week. He will be at the Mt. Zion Campus (Divisadero & Post near Geary). So thank you for the prayers; we are in God's hands, and I know He loves and cares for us. We are hanging on to hope. So many of you continue to pray for us and love us. You all are such a blessing. Debbie...

June 18, 2009

We can make plans, but sometimes they just don't pan out. I don't understand why things happen, but I know I have to take it in stride and take one step at a time. God will lead me and give me the courage and grace to face each day.

Randy had some back pain yesterday and complained about his shirt hurting him. So I felt a lump, thought it was a tumor, but then it could have been an infection. So we went to Alta Bates Emergency, where they lanced the lump and found no signs of infection, so it could be a tumor. So they gave us some antibiotics and sent us home to follow up with UCSF today.

We went to UCSF, and they had to take out the epidural pump, and when they did, we could see where the tubing went to the site of the lump. So, we feel strongly that it's an infection, and not a tumor, however we need to get an MRI to confirm. Since there is an infection, we did not get to put in the intrathecal pump. Instead, we had to admit Randy to a hospital to get IV antibiotics and additional pain meds. I left him about 8 p.m. tonight and I think his nurse (Brad) is on top of the pain schedule. I'll call to check in on him.

We are tabling the intrathecal pump and hopefully can revisit that opportunity in a week to 10 days.

Feel free to visit; he loves the distractions. I don't know for how long he will have to be there. With the weekend coming, I think they might just keep him. I'm taking it one day at a time.

Blessings, Debbie...

Debbie's Thoughts

Using UCSF Pain Management Clinic gave us lots of options and hope. They really gave us every opportunity known to man. Dr. Pasvankas was wonderful. He had many options new on the market for us to try. We were so excited and sure that one of these options would get Randy released from his pain. We did get insurance approval and put in the

Spinal Cord Stimulator. Dr. Pasvankas and team hooked it up to his spine and we turned in on. We didn't see any difference in the pain. We took it home and played with it and didn't see any difference at all.

We then tried an epidural pump, which did give him some release. However, he still had to take the pills on top of it. We had to change out the bag and I even got to go to work with him and change it while he was on the air. He had me wave to the audience. How funny was that? It did end up getting an infection and we did end up putting him in the hospital.

There was a nurse there who decided to "wean" him off his pain meds. This has caused me much grief over the years, and when I think of it, it still makes me mad or cry. We had to put Randy in the hospital for IV antibiotics, so I brought in my pain charts, which I had made on the computer and went over the schedules with the nurses. During the first two shifts, everything went well. He was on the terminal cancer ward, and they were used to high doses of medication.

I woke up the next morning to a call saying that a hospital bed was being delivered to our house. That was odd, but I waited for the bed instead of going to the hospital. I had to clear a path for the bed and move some furniture around in the family room. By the time that got settled, it was 3 PM before I could head out to the hospital.

As soon as I walked in the hospital room, I knew instantly something was terribly wrong. Randy was white as a ghost and shaking. I had never seen him like that before. I asked for his medication log, and the nurse said she was giving someone their insulin and would be right there. Forty minutes later, she still wasn't there. I started yelling and she brought in the chart.

She had only been giving him one eighth of his medications. I went nuts. I explained he was terminal and where his cancer was and that he needed those meds now! While she was out, I went to the desk and asked for a patient advocate. No one came. Then I asked again. No one came. Then I started screaming. I didn't care who heard that no one had given my husband his medication for eight hours. And I kept yelling. They had left him in agonizing pain for eight hours. I wanted a patient advocate, and still no one came. It was amazing to me that no one came to our defense.

I called his doctor, and then I called a friend, asking him to come right away. I told him I may need help getting Randy out of there. The nurse walked in behind me and said, "I wish you would take him home. I'm tired of watching him suffer all day long."

That settled it.

I could have tossed her across the room and out the window. I would have too. It took everything I had not to slap her silly. Steam was blowing out of my ears! Was she a demon? She had made him suffer all day long, and they call her a "nurse"? We don't let dogs suffer like that. Oh my gosh! I got Randy's backpack full of meds, started giving him his medication, called Dr. Pfister, and told him what happened. I had a prescription for antibiotics from the emergency room a few nights before and that tied Randy over for a bit. Finally, Dr. Pfsiter gave me clearance to leave.

My cousin just happened to walk in the room for a visit, and I told him what happened and said, "If it was you, I would pull you out too!"

Dave said, "Thank you!"

We got Randy in a wheelchair. Our friend, Robert, came in to help. I packed everything up and we hauled out of there. It was terrible...just terrible. Just as I hit the door, the head nurse came in and begged me to stay. I said, "There is no way!" I didn't curse. Randy never spoke of that incident and would not let me speak of it in his presence. It was a very traumatic experience for him.

When I think about this time that Randy stayed in the hospital for pain management, I had hoped the doctors would knock him out for a day or two so he would get some rest. But instead, it was medications every two hours, like at home, and finally we got a nurse who thought she was going to "wean" him off his meds. Yes, she thought he was taking too much pain medications. She was right! Randy was on a lot of pain medications. However, stage four cancer patients can be in a lot of pain. After watching the first day, I thought the nurses were keeping him comfortable and on track. Thank God we got a hospital bed.

Never leave your loved one alone. Have someone who is familiar with the pain regiment present all the time and make sure the nurses are on schedule. We had all his pain medications in his backpack at the hospital, but we were told not to give him any. In case something happens, they need to know exactly what he had taken.

But when it all went sideways, I got extremely angry. I wasn't polite and sweet. I screamed for a patient advocate. I never got a patient advocate since they didn't work on weekends. When I called the hospital to find a patient advocate, I was transferred over to a public relations person who said she was a patient advocate. However, the public relations person works for the hospital and not the patient. I was "handled." I won't go back to that hospital, and I will make sure that I don't leave someone alone, even if a hospital bed is coming to the house.

I wasn't given any answers why this happened. Someone did tell me the nurse was from a different department, and it was the Head Nurse's first day. I believe she must have come from the Satan Division. I am still upset over this situation even as I write this. This hospital has an excellent reputation. Randy should have been comfortable and getting the best treatment. A good friend had successful open heart surgery there, and we were confident that Randy would receive excellent care. This was a tough lesson to learn. When it's critical, someone must stay with your loved one, even if every confidence is given. You never know when the wrong nurse will walk through those doors. When I called—well, actually screamed—for a patient advocate, I never got one. We just had to remove Randy and take him home.

The following is a letter I sent to the pain management hospital in response to a bill I received from them:

July 16, 2009

Re: Randy Clemmons 6/18, 6/19 & 6/20/09

Yesterday, I received a notice from Blue Cross, that they were billed and was paying on Randy's care during 6/18 - 6/20/09. I am very surprised that billing wasn't put on hold until after your investigation of the torture that Randy endured while under the hospital's care. Randy, a stage 4 mesothelioma patient, was put in your care to manage his pain after an infection from an epidural pain pump. It was made very clear upon his arrival at the hospital his current medication needs. I don't know what happened from Thursday & Friday to Saturday, but Randy suffered from a lack of communication or a nurse who decided not to take care of the pain.

Randy won't even let anybody talk about his stay at the hospital in his presence. It was so traumatic for him. It was the most pain he has been in since his battle with cancer while under the care of your nurse. Randy kept pushing the nurse's button and begging for more pain medication and she would just bring him the "little bit" she felt he needed, when for months and months he has been on high doses of narcotics to help with the pain. Randy's case was exceptional and it was explained thoroughly by myself to the admitting nurse the amount of pain medication he would need to keep him stable and the purpose of having him there.

When I came in on Saturday at 5:45 p.m., Randy was shivering in pain in a chair next to his bed. I asked immediately for the medication log and it took the nurse 40 minutes to bring the log to me and another 10 minutes for her to get the medication to him. It was about 6:50 PM when she came in with his medication. His medication was reduced for eleven hours and he was suffering the most he ever suffered for eleven hours (I repeat) in horrific pain. I believe he was starting withdrawal symptoms by this time.

The nurse said she wished I would take him home because she was tired of watching him suffer all day. She knew he was suffering "all day," and she didn't bother to give him enough medication to give him relief. I don't believe she knew he was stage four. He has cancer on his heart, esophagus, diaphragm, and lung. It was the whole purpose of having him in the hospital in the first place was so he wouldn't suffer, so his pain would be managed. Well, your staff failed, failed big time. Why wasn't the floor nurse called in or a head nurse to evaluate the situation?

You are our advocate, aren't you? I expect you to fight for Randy! At least hold off on the billing until this situation has been resolved. He has been in horrible pain since 8/21/08 when seen in your emergency room. He has been treated at your Cancer Center since 1/07/07. His diagnosis and surgery was done by your surgeon in your hospital in December of 2006. All of his PET scans are in your computers...including a detailed report of pain medications he was on as of 6/17/09 when we took him to your emergency room. Therefore, you have Randy's history. Also, to top it all off, I gave a detailed and thorough explanation when we checked him in. I don't believe you understand the gravity of how much Randy suffered and how angry I am that I trusted Randy to your care. It should have never happened! We took every precaution. We need answers and action!

Waiting on your report,

Debra Clemmons

Cc: President of Hospital

(At present time, 4 years and still waiting for the report.)

Top Row: Lynn Lyle, Diane Lubcyiks, Jane Goldspring,
Jean Small, Lynda Camacho
Front Row: Robin Tigh, Debbie Clemmons, Tammy
Christensen, Linda Dahl, Randy Clemmons

Chapter 17: Goodbye to KFAX

Actual Internet Updates

July 18, 2009

I have to say, God is good! Randy was able to celebrate Brady's 18th birthday with us. To top it all off, the Taylor's were "BBQ-ing," and we went to their house for dinner and to sing happy birthday. So now Brady is a man. However, I'm not so sure...maybe a "teenier." He really does have some more growing up to do. When do boys mature? However, I was so happy to have Randy here with us to witness this event.

Since Randy came home from UCSF, he has had a bad headache and unable to keep food down for the past week. He did lose some more weight. We ended up back at UCSF today where Dr. Pasvankas ended up putting in a blood patch in the spine to help seal a vacuum that would help the headache. So far, he still has a headache (which might take a day or two), but the bit of food he's eaten is able to keep down.

We ordered a PCA pump last Monday. However Dr. Pfister wrote the orders, but not on official script and went on vacation. The pharmacy wouldn't fill it until he gets back. We tried many different ways to find a doctor to rewrite the orders, but no success. However, today, bless her heart, Megan at the Alta Bates Cancer Center was able to find another doctor to write the orders and sent it to Sutter Home Care. Sutter Home Care gave Randy's Sunday appointment install to someone else, because they didn't have the official prescription. Hopefully someone will come in Monday morning and access his port and get the pain pump running. This will allow us to sleep at night. Randy has had to get up and take pain pills through the night since August. If he sleeps through the scheduled time, then he wakes up in awful pain.

Is it just us? Or do other people in this situation have to fight for every little thing? I feel like every time I turn around, we have another glitch, another problem to solve, another door to kick down, another road block. Just trying to get morphine for him was a nightmare, one day, when I found out that Wellness RX, a prescription approval system, is in the Philippines, and they weren't going to authorize Randy's morphine. How does that work? They aren't even Americans in America! And they get to pull rank over Dr. Pasvankas on how much morphine Randy can have? There has to be a better system for stage four cancer patients who are terminal. No one should ever have to suffer in so much pain at the end of their lives.

So if you would like to pray for us, we need this blood patch to work and Randy's headaches to clear up and he can keep food down. We really need that pain pump and the sooner the better.

I did leave a message with Sutter Home Care. If there are any cancellations or any way we could get this pump sooner than Monday morning…Randy really needs a break. So say a prayer and hopefully my next update will be full of good news.

Blessings to you all, Debbie…

July 22, 2009

Just to give an update: no headaches since the blood patch or nausea. We did get the pain pump installed yesterday, but not enough medication is running through yet to keep Randy out of pain.

We had a very painful night last night with no sleep. We are walking zombies. I was able to bump up the pain meds last night over the phone with the pharmacy. We had two nurses bump up the pump today, but he still is in pain. Sometimes it takes a while if you get behind the pain to catch up with it.

Boys have dentist appointments tomorrow and Garrett has an infected ingrown toenail. Yes, we went through this many times with Brady and will have to have Garrett's cut out next Monday morning and hopefully kill the root. So things are happening! Oh boy!

I told Randy if he got his weight up to 150 lbs, naked, and pain under control, he could go back to work at KFAX. He says he knows it is radio, but he should have some clothes on. ;P Blessings, Debbie...

July 23, 2009

Hey, just to let you know where we are.

We had a nurse come in last night and disconnect the PCA pain pump. Randy's pain had increased so much with the pump that Monday and Tuesday nights he was in more pain (levels 7 & 8) and we kept increasing the morphine until he was getting 150mg/hr and 75/mg 3 x an hour. Through an IV, this is an incredible amount. So we were adding pills back to the mix, and then decided for some reason that the pump wasn't doing what was expected of it. So the answer isn't morphine.

We were thinking that maybe a methadone drip might be the solution, but we just got a call from UCSF saying that it would be too toxic to the heart. I don't think they make a methadone pump. However, every time we switch out the methadone and increase morphine, Randy's pain increases.

We went back to our regiment of "pills" 15 times a day. But he's able to get sleep, two hours at a time. Monday and Tuesday he got four hours total for the two days. So I'm going to let him sleep as much as possible today.

We have a system since school is out. Brady gets dad up at 1 & 3 a.m., and I get him 5 & 7 a.m. This way we each get a block of sleep. Now if I can get my hot flashes to coordinate in the time frame, we will have it made.

I think by this afternoon (Thursday), Randy will be feeling better and up to visitors and calls. Or even tomorrow will be better. Blessings to all, Debbie...

Debbie's Thoughts

Saying Good Bye to KFAX was difficult for Randy. July 9, 2009 was Randy's last day. He remained on the air as long as he could. He wanted to honor the Lord and give Him all the glory. As long as what he was doing was of excellence, he wanted to do it. There came a point where the pain medication was clouding his judgment, making it difficult for him to compensate or troubleshoot mix-ups or problems on the air. That's when he knew he needed to resign from his position.

However, I did pick up Randy for his last day on the air as he said goodbye to his station where he had the time of his life. This is where he took your calls and interviewed so many musicians and authors. It broke all our hearts to say goodbye to the family he loved so much at the station. I hear rumors that his voice stills echoes the halls throughout the station. I think, of course, that is where he would be.

We also got to know the most wonderful family, the Taylors. Their son Jake is good friends with Garrett. He is like a third son to me. I love that boy. He is so bubbly and full of joy. The family came over for a BBQ or two in the year or so before Randy's passing. They have been a great support and good friends. We didn't have any celebrations for Brady's graduation or birthday because of Randy's pain, the pain pumps, and hospitals and clinics. Brady thought it would just be too much extra to put on us. So the Taylors "just happened" to invite us over for a BBQ at their house on Brady's birthday. Kevin got some meat! And I asked if I could bring a cake and we could sing "Happy Birthday" to Brady. No problem. Randy now can say he was at Brady's 18th birthday party.

When Randy was diagnosed with cancer, we weren't sure Randy would see this day, so we were very pleased just to not only see him there, but to enjoy it with our friends. Kevin and Dara were there for us after Randy's passing, always lending a hand, giving us rides, going to the store, and picking up kids. They kept the boys for me when my mom was put on life support and passed away. Kevin has continually reached out to the boys after their dad passed away. I know that Kevin has hit his knees more than once for this family, Thank you, Taylors.

As far as pain pumps went, none of them ever worked. It was because of the type of medications that could be placed in them were of a morphine nature. Methadone seemed to do better than morphine, so I got to thinking that methadone was the answer. I called Dr. Pasvankas and he said that amount of methadone would be too toxic. I then called Dr. Pfister and found out that methadone doesn't go into a pump device. Later, when we called in hospice, the doctor working with the team recommended decreasing the morphine and increasing the methadone. After a point additional amounts of morphine becomes ineffective. It worked. Unfortunately, Randy only had one day of pain relief before he passed. I think the amount of methadone that Hospice put Randy on, 600 mg, was too much, too fast, or possibly toxic.

If you are going through difficulties getting pain under control, ask your doctor to consider the methadone, but maybe stair-step up the dose. I wish we had figured this out about a year earlier. It seemed that Dr. Jessop had us on the right track, just not enough of it.

Randy loved having visitors. Often our house was filled with company just sitting and watching a ball game or sitting on the back deck drinking ice tea. It was so wonderful to sit back and relax and just enjoy our time with one another. Friends and family from out of town would just stop by and say, "Hi." Everybody was welcomed, and I'd even be coloring my hair when people dropped by. I didn't care. We had our doors opened and we were so blessed by having friends and family over. I am so glad we had that time together.

Thoughts on the Intrathecal Pain Pump:

After a week of treating the infection from the spinal pump, we were approved for the intrathecal pump to be installed. It also goes into the spine at a deeper level than other solutions. Randy was in the hospital overnight and there should have been instant relief with its installation. However, we had morphine pumping in and he was still taking pain pills by mouth, so Dr. Pasvankas took him off the pump and we came home. Our last recourse is a PCA pump. We called homecare and they agreed to come to our house to help Randy put in a pain pump.

When the pump was taken out of the spine, Randy had a terrible headache. Placing the pump broke a seal in the spinal cord, which can cause a terrible headache. We had to go back in and have a blood patch placed. Once the patch was in place, his headache was released.

Randy was put to sleep while they put on the blood patch. I was sitting next to him when he woke up. He looked at me and said, "My side hurts."

I said, "Oh, they had to access your port."

He said, "No, the other side."

I asked him, "You mean where your cancer is?"

He then asked, "I have cancer?" He had forgotten he had cancer. He then started singing, "I can see clearly now."

How funny he could be, making light of his situation. He came home feeling much better and started eating a bit more.

I can't hear that song on the radio without seeing him lying on that table and causing me to cry. I have some relief now, because I know he is out of pain and suffering. We didn't know it at the time, but it seemed that attacking Randy's pain through his spine wasn't the answer. Later, closer to his death, we found that it was methadone that released him from the pain, not the morphine and opium products.

As Randy got deeper and deeper into his pain, he turned more and more into His relationship with God for comfort. There is a point that the pain gets so bad with no release that your only hope is God and you tap into that supernatural power. He kept his eyes on the goal, and he wanted to do his best to bring the glory to God in whatever he had left here to do. He asked me to order a print of Jesus in heaven hugging a saint who just came to the gate. We hung that where Randy could focus in on it. That was the goal, seeing Jesus face to face. He knew where he was headed, and he was on his way there.

Whatever you do, do it all for the glory of God. – 1 Corinthians 10:31

In the end, it's not the years in your life that count. It's the life in your years. – Abraham Lincoln.

Chapter 18: August 2009 Time at Home

Internet Updates

August 2, 2009

Here we are in August. We couldn't have made it without you guys. Everywhere I turn, we are surrounded by friends and encouragement. We are so blessed to have each of you in our lives. Each of you played a role in keeping us strong.

Randy continues to be in pain. However, it has subsided some in the past day. We have increased his methadone, and once the pain is under control, we can decrease his morphine. He's taking way too much morphine. I am, once again, battling for his meds, waiting for prior authorization. It's enough to make you nuts! Nuts! Nuts! I have a contact at the insurance company, which I will call tomorrow, and see if she can help us out.

We met with hospice, and Randy is still getting around, taking showers, going to church, saw Star Trek last weekend, visits with friends, so we are going to wait a bit more before calling them in…when he can't get around.

The boys will leave for camp next Sunday, Aug 9th, and will be gone for a fun filled week of working! It will be good for them. They are going to Hume Lake Christian Camp with Ron Kennedy and gang. We need to get Garrett's toe healed up well. He told me he's really wrapping it at camp so dirt doesn't get in it. He doesn't want to go through an infected, ingrown toenail again.

We have had a few people come and spend the night. This has been a huge help. It allowed my brain to function the next day without cobwebs floating around, and Randy could get the help he needed. So our biggest thanks to you watchmen. Randy says he feels better, knowing someone else is nearby.

Okay, no word from us is good news. We don't have any big plans for the week except going to KFAX on Wed for a quick get together with Randy's coworkers. I'll touch base in a week or so.

We are so lucky to have each of you and count you as a blessing. Blessings to you all, Debbie...

August 11, 2009

Today Hospice came in and took over the medication woes. The difficulties in getting pain medication really had me singing the blues last week. I even called the State Insurance

Commissioner's Office for assistance. After the fourth time, the authorization unit in the Philippines denied Randy's medication and filed an independent review. They can't even make any outbound calls to the pharmacy, doctors, cancer center or patient. Then everything gets sent to the wrong place. They say it's approved by the doctor, but then it doesn't go through! What a mess! With Hospice, all I have to do it pick up the medication at the pharmacy and everything is approved. No more authorizations! Yippee!

Randy is still getting medication around the clock every two hours, but hopefully, Hospice may be able to spread that out some. Randy is getting a bit spoiled by having "friends" spend the night and give him his medication. He said that even if Hospice spreads out the times, he still wants over-nighters to come and hang with him. He's like a Junior Higher with sleepovers.

His appetite needs to improve some and his weight is still down. He is in good spirits and enjoys, really enjoys company. So thank you all take the time to come by and say, "Hi."

Boys are at camp with Ron Kennedy and gang on the work crew. I hope having some good times. I am sure, very sure, being "razzed" by the gang as well. We were blessed by a gift from a KFAX listener to be able to pay for the boys to go to Hume Lake. They didn't even know us, never met Randy, but sent a gift, and we used it to give the boys a chance to help and do good works.

Randy gets out here and there. We saw the movie, "Julia & Julie," yesterday (it was a hoot), went out for Chinese food, and the grocery store today. We went to two church services on Sunday. We had a real experience at Hilltop Community Church where a guest pastor from Gilroy, CA, gave his awesome testimony and his personal battle with cancer. God is truly amazing, and it's incredible the pastor was there to tell his story and offer hope. He offered prayer and we went right down for an anointing.

Okay, we are hanging on. Come by and visit, spend the night, come and Randy watch, call any time after 10:00 a.m. is a good time. He has rough nights getting his meds every two hours and sleeps in a bit in the mornings. Blessings, Debbie...

Debbie's Thoughts

We were blessed by some night watchmen that came while the boys were at camp and stayed with us while Brady and Garrett went to Hume Lake to work at the camp with Ron

Kennedy and his crew. Someone would come and stay with me so I could sleep, and they would give Randy pills when an alarm would go off. It was wonderful not to be alone all through the night. I was running on adrenaline most of the time and was so exhausted. My ears were tuned in to every sound Randy would make through the night…like a mother to her newborn. If Randy would groan, I would be up, checking the time and the pills to make sure we were on schedule. It was like a sixth sense. When the watchmen would come, I'd try and go to the furthest room in the house, so I wouldn't hear. It didn't matter. I'd hear him anyway. Heiti put this together for us. Thank you, Heiti.

I feel, even though hospice was great in bringing in his meds so I didn't have to fight Blue Cross anymore for pain meds, the methadone increase was way too much, too fast. I believe we didn't need to go from 40 mgs to 600 mgs instantly. That really was a huge increase. They did take out a lot of morphine products and justified the increase by saying the amount of narcotics would be about the same, only a different type. I often wondered.

The boys came home from camp for only a week before Randy's passing. They regretted the time spent away from their dad, but I let them know that their dad was glad they were out and about doing good works instead of just sitting around "looking" at him. I told them that he loved them very much and enjoyed every minute they had together. I think if we had a crystal ball and we knew the day he would pass, we would have done things differently. But the boys have good memories with their dad at Hume Lake. Randy had baptized Brady in that lake a few years earlier.

They needed to get away, however. They had spent most of the summer sitting around with their dad, watching baseball, DVD's, and movies. Mostly, Randy would just fall asleep, leaving the boys to watch by themselves, so it was good they went off to camp for a week.

He is not the God of the dead, but of the living, for to Him all are alive. – Luke 20:30

Chapter 19: Randy Brady Clemmons

August 19, 2009

Randy Brady Clemmons is now broadcasting in the heavenly realms. His deep and passionate bass voice is echoing throughout the streets of gold. He was a beacon of light, even while fighting a tumultuous battle with cancer for the past two and half years.

Randy Brady was the morning host of KFAX (The Spirit of the Bay), bringing hope to a lost and fallen world. He passed away surrounded by family and friends and entered the arms of Jesus. His suffering and pain have now ended, and he has a new and glorious body. His voice has been restored, and he is singing God's praises with the saints and angels.

Born at Herrick Hospital in Berkeley, CA, Randy grew up in Rollingwood, El Sobrante. He attended Rancho Elementary School, Helms Jr. High School, and De Anza High School where he graduated in 1973. Later, he attended the Columbia School of Broadcasting.

While growing up on Rollingwood Dr., he kept horses at Hobb's stable. He was a member of First Baptist Church in Richmond for 42 years and NorthShore Community

Church. Randy sang with the Forever Family Gospel Group, 4 Given Quartet, and Sound of Joy. He was often a guest soloist with various church choirs.

He worked at Kerr Mfg in Emeryville for 19 years, Covance for 6 years, and then pursued his passion and broadcasted with KECG, KJOY, The Bridge and KFAX. He hosted the Christian Fellowship days with the San Francisco Giants and Oakland A's and hosted many local concerts and events.

He is survived by his wife of 24 years, Debbie; sons: Brady & Garrett; mother and stepfather: Juanita & Orin Wakefield, sisters and brothers: Cheryl Palmieri, Jody (Richard) Stratford, Colleen (John) Kelley, Jean Wakefield, Anne (Greg) Bowser, Beth (Norm) Holly, Orin Robert (Susanne) Wakefield, Chuck and Liz Hubbell, Richard & Barbara Freed, David & Michelle Freed, Paul & Monica Freed and Chris and Tonia Hubbell, Marianne and Steve Bowling; and numerous nephews and nieces, grand nephew and nieces. He was preceded by his father Johney and brother-in-law Gordon Palmieri.

A memorial service will be held at Hilltop Community Church in Richmond on Saturday, September 5, 2009 @ 2:00 p.m., where we will celebrate the life of Randy Brady

Clemmons. Please dress brightly and bring your smile and "Randy-isms."

Debbie's Thoughts

I thought about leaving this out, until one day at church the guest speaker told us how God wanted us to be real. How our testimony had to include the good, the bad, and the ugly. How we are human and how important it is to share how we handle things in our human nature. So I decided to include this as well. You may want to skip the rest of this chapter and that's okay. The rest of this is pretty painful to read.

However, it's also good to include it so you'll know what to expect and to prepare for if you face similar situations.

When we signed up with hospice, we were told *not to call 911* if Randy had an emergency. We had a DNR and there really was no point. However, in hind sight, that was exactly what we should have done. If your hospice cannot control the pain or someone unqualified it taking care of your loved one, **call 911!** It would have been better for Randy to die comfortably in a hospital than to have the nightmare we had to endure. We didn't have much luck with the hospitals in the past in controlling Randy's pain, but I think anything might have been better than the way he died.

Even if you have hospice, if you need more help, call 911.

The following is a letter written to Hospice, detailing my frustration and anger:

August 27, 2009

RE: Randy Clemmons (Lack of Treatment on 8/18/09 & 8/19/09)

Words cannot describe how horrible last Tuesday night was for us. It was such a nightmare. We hired Hospice so Randy wouldn't die in agonizing pain like his father. I told Randy over and over again not to worry, because we would have Hospice. It was a joke! Such incompetence!

When Randy started seizing about 6:30 p.m. on 8/18, I called Hospice and left a message. Then a nurse called, saying they were sending someone out. Randy was not responsive, but groaning in pain and jerking. The Hospice nurse didn't come until almost 10 PM! By that time, we had called Dr. Pfister, and we dissolved Ativan, and Randy finally relaxed. This nurse didn't call the 24 hours pharmacy and get us any liquid medication. We didn't even know there was a 24 hour pharmacy for this kind of a thing until 2:30 AM. I'm still waiting for the meds. We had to dissolve Randy's pills in water, put it in a syringe, and put it in the back of his mouth.

The nurse left, and Randy continued to seize and jerk several episodes through the night. At 1 AM, Randy started again. I called Hospice and they said a nurse would call back.

While waiting for the call back, 1 mg of Ativan wasn't working and we called Dr. Pfister, and he said to make it 2 mg of Ativan every ½ hour. I was also dissolving morphine and Norco to help with the pain. When the Hospice Nurse called on the phone, she said, "I was all over the place." I hung up. This nurse should have had a printout of all the medication Randy was taking! She was clueless.

My friend Lennette took the next call and said, "No, she hung up on you. She is very frustrated." That was when we learned about the 24 hour pharmacy. Lennette said, "We don't have that; isn't that your job? No we don't have that either. Isn't your job to make sure it's here? No we don't have a nurse here; isn't it your job to make sure that happens?"

I don't understand why someone didn't order Randy medication at 6:30 p.m. when we first called. I don't understand why the nurse on the phone didn't tell me to give him Ativan. The hospice nurse came back about 2:30 a.m. She put a catheter in Randy and we drained almost a liter of fluid (however, only when my nurse friend told her to.) I don't think the nurse knew what to do, but then she left again. She should have never left! Why did she leave? That nurse didn't know the hospice she worked for had liquid medication or that compassion kits were suppose to be given.

Randy started seizing and groaning in pain again about 4 a.m., and continued until he died at 7:26. We called hospice at 4 a.m., but the nurse was tired and their other nurse couldn't come out till after 8 a.m., because she had to get a baby sitter. No one ever came back. Even till this day! No one ever came to give the time of death, nothing! We never got the medication Randy needed, and he died in horrible pain. It was so bad. Randy suffered for 13 hours. We didn't have a compassion kit, liquid meds, things that would have calmed and taken him out of pain.

1.) We need a formal apology from management.

2.) We should not be charged for such torture.

3.) We need to know that steps are being taken to prevent this from happening to someone else.

4.) We need to know that the nurses have patient information on medications when taking calls. I gave a spreadsheet to every nurse that walked in the house. Everybody should have known the elaborate needs of Randy's care.

5.) We need to know that "compassion kits"

are given to every patient.

6.) We need timelines and completion dates confirming when the above steps will be done.

This experience will be forever etched in my brain. The images of his pain and suffering will stay with me for a life time. His moaning and groaning will forever echo in my ears. I just can't believe the lack of consideration and care. It's so unbelievable, horrible, and inconceivable. My children will always know their dad suffered a tragic death, and it could have been prevented. The impact of this event will forever haunt Randy's family and friends.

Extremely disappointed,

Debra Clemmons

The following is Lennette's Letter to Hospice after observing what had happened to Randy:

August 28th, 2009

To Whom It May Concern:

When one thinks of Hospice, one thinks of comfort during the last days of one's life. One thinks of a sense of peace for family and friends and of help and care during the most difficult transitions in life. This was not the case the last days of Randy Clemmons life.

The Hospice care for Randy was truly lacking. Hospice did not equip the family to help Randy transition from this world to the next. This was the first time Mrs. Clemmons had to face death. She had hoped not to do it alone. She had hoped to have the help of an organization who knows death, who sees it daily, and understands it, an organization that takes pride in giving comfort to those who are leaving this world and their families.

Apparently, there is a comfort kit filled with medicines that would have helped Randy transition with less pain and to help with any seizures and build up of mucus in the air passage. One would think that this comfort kit would have been provided the very day Hospice started. The comfort kit was never given to Mrs. Clemmons. The last 13 hours of Randy's life could have been more comfortable, but it was not. The pain seemed unbearable as Randy moaned throughout the night. A little education on what to expect and what each medicine was for would have helped tremendously, but the education and medication was never provided.

The first seizure lasted at least 1 hour as Mrs. Clemmons held on to her dying husband, not knowing how to help him. This was of course the first call she made to Hospice. After an hour and a half of not hearing from Hospice, Mrs. Clemmons called again and was told the nurse was on her way. We then received a call from the nurse who stated she was on her way to a death to release a body and that she would be there as soon as she was done. Where was she the hour and a half before the death? Where was she when Mrs. Clemmons was afraid and uncertain? Where was she when Randy was having a seizure in his chair for at least an hour and all Mrs. Clemmons could do was hold him? Where was the comfort kit that had the anti-seizure medicine?

Finally, close to 3 hours after Mrs. Clemmons' initial call, the nurse arrives. Did she bring a comfort kit? No. Did she bring liquid methadone? No. Did she bring anything or leave anything at all? Only two small syringes for Mrs. Clemmons to administer medicine—not comfort, not a sense of peace, not any instruction. She took Randy's pulse. She helped administer one dose of medication of which we dissolved tablet forms of morphine in water and injected into his cheek. Did she tell us there was a 24 hour pharmacy that could bring us liquid meds? No. She then left. She left without leaving any briefs, chucks, or swabs. She left without giving us any idea of what to expect or what to do. Randy had not passed fluids since before 5 that evening. Did she address that? No. She left without leaving us the comfort kit or any comfort.

Just 4 hours later Mrs. Clemmons is on the phone again with Hospice. It is now 1 in the morning. Randy is having his 4th or 5th seizure and still has not passed any fluids. There is uncertainty everywhere. None of us felt equipped to handle the situation. All of us felt a burden for Randy and his pain. All of us had hoped for help.

Mrs. Clemmons was trying to explain the situation to the Hospice triage nurse, however due to the stress of the situation she had to hang up and go to her husband who needed her, instead of sit on the phone and answer questions from triage. When triage called back, she thought they had been disconnected when, in reality, Mrs. Clemmons just hung up the phone.

At that point, I spoke to the nurse on the phone. The nurse asked me, "Why don't you have liquid methadone?" I responded, "You tell me. Don't you provide it?" The liquid medication was supposed to be delivered Tuesday morning; however it was not, for reasons I do not know. She informed me there was a 24 hour pharmacy and she had to decide if it was best to call them immediately or wait till morning. She decided to wait until morning— which of course was too late.

During these phone calls, we asked that a nurse be sent out again. A friend of ours was concerned that some of Randy's pain was being caused by his bladder being full and he was unable to release the urine. So we requested that the nurse bring a catheter. She did and emptied approximately 2 liters of fluid from his bladder. Did she bring or leave a comfort kit? No. And so for the rest of the morning, the rest of Randy's life, he suffered. He suffered until he passed on to the next world.

Randy's suffering has ended, but it is his family who still suffers today. What if they had had the comfort kit? Randy's suffering would have been less. What if they had had adequate help from Hospice? Randy would have transitioned more peacefully. Yes, Randy is at peace now, but his family will forever remember the fear, the feeling of inadequacy, and the pain of watching him suffer his last hours with them. This could have been prevented.

Sincerely,

Lennette K. LaRiza

How can words ever express the horror of that night? It was so difficult to get the help we so desperately needed. There is so much regret, sadness, hopelessness, and the pure panic of not being able to help. I had just given Randy some apple pie that his cousin Elaine had brought over, and he wanted some tea with it. I handed him the glass and he spilled it. No worries. I went to get him some dry clothes. When I got back, he said something very odd, "Isss thisss the traaiiin to Oakland?" and then, "Lassst stop for Ashby."

I looked at him and said, "Do you think you are on BART?" That is when I called hospice and asked for help. Then I called his sister, Colleen, who lived the furthest away. It would take her almost three hours to drive here. I wasn't sure what I had to deal with, but if it was serious, I wanted Randy's family here. I grabbed the phone, called for some friends to come over to help me, got behind Randy, and held him while he trembled and jerked. I didn't know what else to do.

When Lennette arrived, she asked if she could call a friend of ours. I said, "Yes!" I can't share her name since she didn't work for this hospice company. This friend shared a room with me on more than one occasion at Women of Faith. She was a hospice nurse and it "just so happened" that it was her day off. She came right over. Lennette started looking for the compassion kit and asking me where it was. "What compassion kit?" I demanded. "We never got one."

An hour passed and no hospice. My friend, the hospice nurse, arrived and also began asking for the compassion kit— which we didn't have. I did have Ativan, but we had to liquefy it. We called Dr. Pfister, who could hear Randy in the background, and he told us how much to give him. Then we called him back and he told us how much more we could give; Still no hospice had come. We finally got Randy calmed down, and just then the boys walked in the door. They had been shopping. Randy sat up, and in a voice clear as a bell, said, "Brady, Garret." The boys went into the bedroom.

I had wanted Brady to go and pick up one of Randy's sisters, but I had just learned that she was still out of town. Still, we had his family praying for us. I then called Randy's mom and stepdad and they came right over. It was a good time to come, because we had gotten Randy quiet and he wasn't seizing anymore. Randy's mom was able to sit next to him and hold his hand and comfort him. Randy's youngest sister, Colleen, arrived along with some friends of ours.

Hospice finally arrived about 10 PM, four hours after the first call. However, we had already given Randy enough meds through the syringe to keep him calm for a time. The nurse came in without any medication, no compassion kits, and no knowledge on how to get any help for him if this started up again.

We used the time to tell stories of old. We got a hymn book out and sang some hymns. Ron Kennedy called, and we held the phone up to Randy's ear so Ron could talk to him. My brother-in-law, John, was around keeping the boys company. Family and friends were helping figure out how to manage Randy's pain and seizures. We let Uncle John sleep in my bed because he worked all day and was so tired. Donny and Buster, two of Randy's best buddies, stayed the night here with us and helped me get Randy to the hospital bed to lay him down. A few more friends would drop by and visit for a bit.

I remember turning the pills into liquid so I could get them in a syringe and putting them down the side of his throat.

I kept saying, "One more time." Of course, I'd have to keep doing it over and over, each time I'd say, "One more time."

At one point, Randy's muffled and quiet voice said, "One more time."

It let me know that, even though he was seizing, he was still there with us. I was glad because I knew he could understand what was happening and we were doing everything in our power to help him.

The hospice nurse, not my friend, was dressed for a party, and I think she was anxious to get to it. She left and came back once. She wasn't trained and didn't know where or how to get medication for us. Randy's mom left around midnight, and I am so grateful for that because it was about one in the morning when Randy started seizing again. It would have been terrible for his mom to see that. She was already torn apart to see him with cancer, but if she had seen this, it would have been agonizing for her.

Again, we had no hospice nurse during this battle and then, at two in the morning on the phone with hospice, we found out there is a 24 hour pharmacy! Why on earth didn't that party nurse call anything in for us? We called Dr. Pfister again for advice on the pain meds and how much to give him. We were in such a state and it was such torture not to be able to calm Randy down quickly.

After we managed to calm Randy down this second time, someone—I can't remember who—told me to take a nap, so I did for a bit, and got back up after a few hours. Randy was still moaning with every breath. I went to make coffee, and my friend said, "The time is near."

His breathing had changed. So I went to Randy's side and told him, "I love you." He said, back to me, muffled, "I love you." Those were the last words he spoke.

I woke up Brady, told him to come say goodbye to his dad. He came in the family room and collapsed all at once in a dead faint. Randy's friend's had to pick him up. Brady started crying, stood up on his own, but collapsed again. The guys lifted him up and Brady told his father how much he loved him and what a great dad he was. He lay on the couch near his dad and cried. After a time, Brady turned to me and said, "We need to wake up Garrett."

I said, "You passed out twice. I can't do this to Garrett."

"Garrett needs to be here," he argued.

I thought about it for a minute. I went to Garrett's room, woke him up, and said, "Dad only had a few more minutes. It's up to you, but it's not looking to good. You'll have to be strong and brave if you want to say goodbye."

Garrett got right up, marched right in, went right to Randy's side, and told his dad he was the best dad ever and he will miss him, then he sat next to Brady to wait it out.

Randy's sister, Colleen, tenderly went to her brother and said her goodbyes and then went out to make calls to the rest of the family. The rest of Randy's friends, who were keeping watch, took a turn. He was still with us when everybody said their goodbyes.

Finally, I put my arms around him and said, "It's okay to go. I'll find you." He took his last breath and his spirit was released from his body.

Creedence Clearwater Revival asks the question in a song, "I want to know, have you ever seen the rain, coming down on a sunny day?" Now I can say, "Yes, shining down like water." As the mortuary came and put Randy's body in the back of a van, I knew he was gone. He wasn't there. It was odd, knowing that somehow Randy wasn't in that body anymore. I knew the instant he left. His soul was gone. It was a bright, beautiful, sun shining day. The birds were chirping away like always. There was a squirrel running along the fence, hoping to find a peanut. The sprinklers came on to give the lawn some moisture and the neighbor's newscast could be heard in the background. Normally, we would be making plans to go to a pool or the beach. But here we are left to make plans for a burial, our lives never to be the same. Randy was now in the arms of Jesus and finally out of pain.

In February of 2010, I received a letter from "this reputable hospice group" in response to my own frustrated letter. The letter stated, "Thank you for sharing your concerns. If you have any further questions, please call." I was stunned. After waiting for six months, this is the response we received? So, you bet I called. The woman on the other end of the phone said that she could not discuss the details, however I could trust her that actions were taken. It was not enough for me. I needed to know what actions were taken. I wanted an apology. Randy deserved more, and we most certainly deserved more than that response.

I then tried calling state and county agencies where I could report the lack of care for Randy. It seemed I couldn't find the right agency. I went back and forth between city, state, and county agencies. Until one day, in my doctor's office, a couple of ladies came by and said they were starting a hospice group. So I asked them where I could report the situation we had experienced. They gave me the phone number of the state licensing office. Once I got through, I filed a formal complaint and they researched it. The licensing office validated every single point, executed penalties, people lost jobs, and the hospice group was put on probation. This was a very horrific experience, terrible for me, the boys, Randy's family, and friends who had to go through this ordeal. I wish we had moved Randy to a hospital and had an IV bag of narcotics for him. To end a life this way was terrible and should never be repeated for anybody.

Three years later, a dear friend of mine was going through a difficult time with cancer and pain. I had been very involved in her care and treatments. Her pain got to the point of being difficult to manage—very similar to Randy's. She had been taken to the emergency room to help control her pain. There was some discussion of bringing her back home for the few days and remaining on hospice. However you can't bring that amount of narcotics by IV home to control the pain. So they would have to give her medication by mouth and she was too sedated for that.

After what we went through with Randy's ordeal, I was able to offer counsel without giving details. The family just trusted me. When they read this book, they will fully understand the nightmare they avoided. Since they had already brought her in by ambulance once, the family opted to have her remain comfortable at the hospital. I believe that was a true gift for everybody. No complications, no regrets.

My father passed away ten days after Randy did, and since my brothers were down for Randy's memorial, they took care of all of his details. Eight months after Randy died, our brother-in-law, John, my boy's most favorite uncle who they had silly string, water and frog wars with, was diagnosed with stage-four lung cancer. He passed away a month later. Then soon after that, my mom passed away. It seemed as if all these losses were just bombarding us. Garrett said, "It feels like God is picking on us." Needless to say, our holidays look very different these days.

I thought of what Garrett said, and I realized that God had blessed us, not cursed us. Before we were born, our days are numbered. We don't die before our time…it is always our time! God doesn't turn around in Heaven and react surprised when we arrive there. He doesn't say, "Oh, why are you here?" He is expecting us and receives us. These people in our lives who have passed on were gifts…though some were only given for a very short time. But if they only had one day to be here with us, wouldn't we take it? Wouldn't we take every minute of every day that they could be here? We were lucky!

One day, it will be our turn to leave this life. I hope my family and friends will say, "We were lucky." I think a few might say, "We had a nut." We are all entitled to our opinions.

13For You formed my inward parts; You wove me in my mother's womb. 16Your eyes saw my unformed body; all

216

the days ordained for me were written in your book before one of them came to be. – Psalm 139:13 & 16

God began by making one person, and from him came all the different people who live everywhere in the world. God decided exactly when and where they must live. – Acts 17:26 (New Century Version)

Maybe you have more than one family member sick at one time and you are juggling so many things and responsibilities. Perhaps things are a bit crazy and you are not sure where you should be. I was in that very situation. My mom could have died at any moment and my husband was going through treatments. I know my duty was to my husband and kids, but not to be there when my mom died would have been terrible too. However, God was good and I was there when my mom also passed. I was with her in the ambulance taking her back home to hospice care when she took her last breath. It seemed so odd, one more time; I realized I had taken my first breath with her in an ambulance and she had now taken her last.

If you are in that situation where you feel torn, you'll have to weigh it out and make some hard decisions. You can't be in two places at one time. Just figure out which one is more critical and base it on that.

I can't believe I had three terminally ill family members all at one time. No wonder I couldn't sleep and was such a wreck. My stepdad would say, "When the phone rang, we didn't know what shoe was going to drop." We lived that way for over four years. They say God doesn't give you more than you can handle. I think about that all the time. I always felt this was more than I could handle, and that is why God gave me so many good friends to come along side of me to hold me up. I really am blessed with so many wonderful friends. So if this is you, and in your life you have more than you can handle, get some friends to help hold you up. They won't mind. They will be so grateful it isn't them.

Do you have thoughts of regrets? If you tried a different treatment maybe the outcome would have been successful? Maybe you wonder if you went to Mexico, China, or Germany you could have had a better outcome? Farah Fawcett went to Germany. She fought bravely and had used her considerable resources to do so. We know that Steve McQueen went to Mexico for the apricot seed treatments. He spent a lot of money and he died there.

I didn't know about Dr. Johanna Budwig and "the Budwig Protocol" when we were given our walking papers from the cancer center. We had exhausted all our options. Maybe this program could have worked for Randy like it did for our friend Rick who became cancer free of his pancreatic cancer. He was stage four and the cancer had gone to his liver and stomach. Three months later, he was cancer free. He remains cancer free to this day that I know of. I know this is amazing!

I was asked maybe they got it wrong at UCSF. I don't think so. Dr. Budwig was nominated for seven Nobel Prizes for her research in cancer. She brought thousands of patients to cancer free status and the Budwig Protocol is still being used in Europe, but not so much in the United States to fight cancer. What do we do with these feelings of "Oh, if I had only known? Did I do everything I could? Was there a stone left unturned? Did we jump through all the hoops?" We beat ourselves up all the time and sometimes daily.

The verses above show us we were never in control. God has an appointed time for each of us. He has our place in this earth and His purpose for us. You can let go of the regrets and take hold of His peace. You were never meant to carry that burden. There were doctors in place that tried their best and we did ours. And now God receives our loved one home in heaven. The burden is no longer for us to carry. Jesus will now take that from you and carry that load.

Take My yoke upon you and learn from Me, for I am gentle and humble in heart, and YOU WILL FIND REST FOR YOUR SOULS. For My yoke is easy and My burden is light." – Matthew 11:29-30

After Randy's passing, I kept thinking I needed to get away from home to find peace and rest. With two teenage boys and a Jack Russell at home, I probably did need to get away to think. However, the type of rest I needed was deep in my soul. The pain and emptiness reached so far and so deep into a dark black pit. One day, someone gave me a birthday gift. On the wrapping paper is said, "He will give you rest." It stuck. **He** will *give me rest*. I could quit trying to get away. I was bringing the black pit with me wherever I went. **He** will give me rest. I needed to keep turning to Jesus, and asking Him to *give me rest*. I needed to drink of the Living Water only He can give. It was healing water. I was weary and needed to come to the water to refresh my soul which was crying out tears of grief and loneliness.

The LORD is my shepherd, I shall not want. He makes me lie down in green pastures; He leads me beside quiet waters. He restores my soul; He guides me in the paths of righteousness, For His name's sake. Even though I walk through the valley of the shadow of death, I fear no evil, for You are with me; Your rod and Your staff, they comfort me. You prepare a table before me in the presence of my enemies; You have anointed my head with oil; My cup overflows. Surely goodness and loving kindness will follow me all the days of my life, And I will dwell in the house of the LORD forever. – Psalm 23: 1-6

Chapter 20: The Memorial Service

How wonderful the memorial service was! What a home coming service! It was like we were in heaven. So many people that we hadn't seen in years were there along with the people we saw every day. The church was buzzing with so much excitement.

Randy had asked five people to speak at his service, so I realized this could go on for a long time. I asked each person to keep it to ten minutes...that would put it at an hour. However, Randy did have a few longwinded buddies that did put us over that time limit. By the time we added three praise songs, slide shows, and the speakers, we ended up having a two and a half hour service.

So many people came to help. I believe I wrote over fifty thank-you notes. If I missed you, here are my deepest thanks. My mom and stepdad flew in two days early and went with me to get the flowers and help set up the orchids around the steps and stage. We had an awesome Praise and Worship band come. Precious Perry did such an amazing job with Amazing Grace. Brady wants her to sing it at his service. Well, let's all pray that she lives to a hundred and forty!

In the kitchen, the Taylors, Lennette, and Paula gave a labor of love by preparing and overseeing the refreshments from early morning set up until take down. So many cookies and desserts were brought by so many people that there was enough to supply the church picnic the next day. I got to the reception area when everybody was leaving and there were still so many desserts left. In hindsight, I should have had some sandwiches brought. I just didn't realize how much food people were going to bring.

So many gifts were sent to me, and I used them to help pay for flowers, music, and whatever Randy needed for the service of celebration. Thank you so much for all the gifts of love given.

The church holds about twelve hundred people and it wasn't packed. If you asked the pastor, he'll tell you there were about seven to eight hundred people there. If you ask Randy's mom, she'll tell you that there were over a thousand. No matter how you look at it, the service was well attended. So many KFAX listeners came, and I got to meet many of them after the service. They loved listening to Randy in the mornings. So many friends from all over the state came. I didn't get to see everybody and wish I had the time to do so. He had touched so many lives.

Chapter 21: August 2013 Wrapping It up

Debbie's Thoughts

I was listening to Randy's interview with Craig Roberts and Andy Froiland on KFAX, February 2009, and Randy ends out the program with this, and I'd like to end out the book with it as well:

> "It's all about grace and giving your life to Jesus Christ—you can have eternal life. You can't earn it on your own. Read your Bible; come to know Him. And accept that gift of grace that only He could earn for us.

> "The biggest test for me came that moment when the doctors said to me, 'It's malignant, its mesothelioma, and all we can try to do is keep you comfortable,' and I had no fear. That's when I knew it was real beyond a shadow of a doubt.

> "I have to share this one thing, please, because it excites me so. In Acts, the seventh chapter, verses 54 – 56: *When the members of the Sanhedrin heard this, they were furious and gnashed their teeth at him. But Stephen, full of the Holy Spirit, looked up to heaven and saw the glory of God, and Jesus standing at the right hand of God. "Look," he said, "I see*

heaven open and the Son of Man standing at the right hand of God.'

"Now every other Scripture that you see in the Bible about Jesus in Heaven says He is seated at the right hand of God, but here, as Stephen is about to go into Heaven, he sees Jesus standing at the right hand of God. And we wonder, does He stand to greet Stephen? Does He stand to welcome all of His saints into Heaven? I'll let you know." – Randy Brady

Chapter 22: Randy Tributes

After Randy's passing, KFAX received, I believe, about 500 emails from listeners and fans. Thank you for the encouraging and kind words. Here are just a few of them:

June 2009

Good Morning Randy! ☺

I just wanted to let you know that I continue to keep you and your family in prayer, as you had mentioned to me that they too need prayer. I also wanted to tell you how much you have touched my life in the years that I have been listening to KFAX. You are always a "ray of sunshine" in the morning. I can't wait to turn on my radio at 5:00 a.m. in the morning to hear your voice! ☺ I also wanted to let you know what an inspiration that you have been to me, not just since you have been sick—you have always been an inspiration! ☺ I'm sure that I am not the only one that feels this way and that you have touched many lives through your ministry on the radio.

Thank you Randy for who you are and for your example of faithfulness to the Lord! ☺ I hope to talk to you again after you get out of the hospital. If not, I know where you will be and look forward to seeing you when it is my turn! ☺

In Christian Love…your Sister in Christ,

- Cindy

June 15, 2009

Dear Randy Brady,

We are rooting for you, Randy, and praying that as you have been an inspiration and blessing to us all during your illness you might continue to experience the nearness of our heavenly Father both you and your family. You have been a living example of a Christian under affliction; thank you.

The other morning we chuckled at those little hiccups you had. Keep up the good work; we are with you all the way. You have a vast hoard of listeners that really appreciate you.

- Glenn & Mary, San Jose

June 16, 2009

Dear Randy,

Thank you for your ministry. I've been listening to you for over three years and appreciate your morning joy and you sharing of what's going on in your life. I'm praying for grace and strength and peace for you and your family. Thank you for blessing my life as I struggle with difficult family times. Some days your radio morning show is the highlight of my day and is the reason to wake up and be glad. Thank you also for your sense of humor about your health situation. Yesterday, when you shared about the pain medications and how it is affecting your thoughts, I realized that God has placed you in a job/situation to show us all how we can have victory in this life that we been given. That we can go on with joy and confidence because we KNOW that He is the Author and Finisher of our faith and our very life and breath.

"Your love has given me great joy and encouragement, because you, brother, have refreshed the hearts of the saints." – Phil 7

"God is not unjust: He will not forget your work and the love you have shown Him as you have helped his people and continue to help them:" – Heb 6:10

We love you…

- J. Mosher, San Bruno

July 2009

Dear Randy,

I have enjoyed listening to you every weekday morning while I get ready for work. You have been an inspiration as you shared your faith with the listeners during the progression of your cancer. I am sorry you cannot continue with your work on the air, but God has begun a good work in you. Many seeds have been planted because of your on-air ministry. May God grant you and your family His grace and peace now and always; I will miss your voice.

In Christian Love,

- Carrie

July 6, 2009

Dear Randy,

A few weeks ago on the air, you were talking about how you had to enter the hospital over the weekend because of the extreme pain you were experiencing, and while there, you were reading Philippians 3:10, which says: "I want to know Christ and the power of this resurrection and the fellowship of sharing in his sufferings, becoming like him in his death, and so, somehow, to attain to the resurrection from the dead." You were describing how you are, in fact, sharing in His sufferings (albeit involuntarily) and how our Lord did it for us voluntarily.

That morning, I read Philippians. Through your testimony, the Lord has opened His Word to me like I have never read it before. I have never read the Bible like that before.

Thank you Randy for your ministry and the courage you have in sharing your personal journey. You are my daily prayers. Well done.

Long time listener,

- Greg

July 6, 2009

Randy,

Just writing to let you know what a big part you have played in starting my days in the morning. My alarm is set to KFAX, and it's been a routine to wake up and hear your positive upbeat voice first thing in the morning. I remember the day you announced that you had cancer and that it was incurable. I cried. Through the years, you have become like a friend, and I thank you for sharing your battles and thoughts these last couple of years. I admire your courage and pray for strength, peace, and God's comfort for you and your family.

I will miss hearing you in the mornings, and I hope you know that a lot of people who you will never meet on this side will miss you terribly. I am hoping that you will be back on the air someday. In the meantime, God bless you and your family.

- Geri

July 6, 2013

Good Morning Randy,

Just a quick note to let you know I am praying for you. I have been listening in the mornings before I head to work, and I appreciate your dedication and love of God. Although I will not hear you in the morning, rest assured you are loved and prayed for.

Thank you, Randy.

In His grip,

- Vicki

July 8, 2009

Randy,

I will miss you. Your short reports on your health were a road I traveled with my son just last year. Thank you for letting me pray for you and walk it with you every morning. I look forward to hearing you just as much as hearing Charles Swindoll—and he is good!

Thank you for the blessing your life has been to me and to so many. God bless you, and I pray He will make these next few months a blessing for you and your family. I know it is a very hard road, but Jesus is always there to the end. You will meet my son. You don't know me at all, but we will meet at the foot of Jesus' throne.

Your friend in Christ Jesus,

- M. Sealy

July 9, 2009

Dear brother Randy,

I am continuing to lift you in prayer,

Lovingly,

- Pappa Jay

August 18, 2009

Subject: Thoughts about Randy Brady

Dear Debbie and Family,

Just wanted to let you know how much I enjoyed listening to Randy's upbeat cheerful voice in the mornings. Some days I would feel overwhelmed with life and then I would be blessed by this wonderful announcer who was sick, but one would never know it. Randy has inspired me to stop grumbling and complaining and to instead enjoy life because it is so precious and God has blessed us so abundantly. I will never forget his sense of humor and light-heartedness, and I will look forward to meeting Randy one day in heaven. He lived life to the fullest and he loved people. He was a true example of Christ's love as he touched so many of us with his God-given gifts and talents. I will always remember that courageous voice and that he finished strong doing what he loved…serving the LORD and others.

I will keep you and the children lifted in prayer. God bless you and may the Lord give you strength and comfort always.

- Blessings, Barbara

August 19, 2009

Subject: Remembering Randy Brady

Good Afternoon Craig Roberts!

Thank you for this opportunity to express our love to Randy's wife, Debbie, and their sons, Brady and Garrett. We are grateful that God blessed us to hear Randy's voice on KFAX and also hear him sing occasionally. We did not have an opportunity to meet him personally. Debbie would always share updates with us via email, acknowledging all milestones as blessings from the Lord. She would say, "God be praised" and ended her email updates saying, "In His Grace." Randy was and his wife is still an example of how to live in faith every day; blessings to her and their sons. Thank you KFAX for your ministry of hope to this lost and fallen world.

- The Robinson Family

August 19, 2011

Subject: Randy Brady

I had the pleasure of enjoying Randy Brady and his ministry for all the many years he was at KFAX. Randy started my mornings bright and early with the joy of the Lord—what an inspirational way to begin my day! Randy showed us all how Christians can live with our Lord's love to the very end. I was one of many who participated in praying for Randy and his family. We were made to feel like we were part of one big family, held together with the bond of the Lord. I feel blessed to be able to share with Randy's family my continued prayers for them in their loss and as they are traveling this new season of their lives. Randy is so missed; however, he was so loved and his ministry will continue on in our hearts and souls forever.

233

August 20, 2009

Subject: A Godly Man from My Youth

Debbie,

I so wanted to be there for the memorial service, but it was just not to be. I wanted to share with you and your sons about the man who had a huge impact on my life when I was a youth. He went out of his way to pick me up to take me to softball practice. He spent some extra time trying to get a preteen to lay off the high ones and to stop trying to swing for the fence. Those lessons didn't sink in deep enough until a few years later, but they did sink in. I was a much better player down the road because of his time and patience. I looked up to him for all the 'cool' things he had—cool car, cool laugh and an awesome personality. Mostly his commitment to God!

When I was out there for my Grandpa's funeral, the one person whose story about him I recall was Randy's. I laugh to this day about how he recalled my Grandpa's 'comments' during the games, games I never got to see till that moment, and I got to see them in that quick instant because Randy shared them. I remember going to—I believe it was El Cerrito HS—and sitting with him for his two hour radio show, KECG. At that point, I had been in radio for less than ten years, but he asked me questions with the same intensity as he had answered mine about softball years earlier. When you first started sharing the emails about Randy, I shared them with my listeners here in Wyoming. I shared about how Randy's laugh and voice were something a radio DJ envied. I had a great deal of trouble sharing his passing. It seems, up until then, I failed to realize how much God had moved through him to influence me.

Please share with your sons that, long before Randy was their dad and before he was your husband, he was a man used by God to move me in a particular direction, a godly direction. We all are promised eternity, either in Heaven or Hell. Heaven is a much more pleasant and enjoyable place because Randy is there, having kissed the face of God and danced and sang before Him.

We are told in Ecclesiastes that there is a season for everything. Enjoy every season for what it is, another chance to fully rely and walk with God.

I love you, Debbie, and I hope you will pass along that love to your sons for me.

- Jason Butler (Jaybo Jackson)

August 31, 2009

Hi Debbie—

I received the card recently inviting us to attend the celebration of Randy's life on September 5th. Unfortunately, that weekend I will be far away from the S.F. area. Otherwise, I assure you, that I would have been honored to attend. In a small way, I was able to experience some of the celebration as I tuned into the radio broadcast the other day to hear you and others give your thoughts on Randy and recollections of his life both in earlier days and more recent times.

I'd like to say that is was truly a special experience to get to know you and Randy over the course of the past year. By the nature of my job, I am often put in the situation of only getting to know people in what can be the darkest and hardest of times. Fortunately, that also enables me to see some truly amazing things from people in those situations. To see Randy's courage, his perseverance, and his contagiously positive attitude under such duress was awe inspiring. The same goes for your tireless work on Randy's behalf and the love, strength, and commitment that the two of your shared.

My thoughts have been, and continue to be, with you and all at these difficult times.

Best,

- George

Chapter 23: How to Choose an Asbestos Attorney

By Steven Kazan

How I Met the Clemmons:

On December 29, 2006, I was sitting in my office when I got a call from our receptionist. She told me that there was a Mr. Randy Clemmons on the phone wanting to speak with me and asked if I could take the call. I said yes. When I answered the phone, a voice said, "Hello, Steven. This is Randy Clemmons. Do you remember me?" And that's how my involvement with Randy's illness and the resulting litigation began.

I did remember Randy, although it had been almost 35 years since we first became acquainted, and I hadn't heard from him in a very long time. Randy became my client in 1982. His father, Johney Joseph Clemmons, had spent 30 years working at the Fibreboard Corporation's Emeryville, California asbestos insulation manufacturing plant. Johney began to get sick in the early 1970s, and by 1975 had severe pulmonary asbestosis, a scarring of the lungs caused by asbestos fibers that restricted the lungs' ability to provide enough oxygen to the body.

He continued to work until 1977 when he could no longer manage, and at age 57 was forced to retire. Several years later, he developed lung cancer on top of his asbestosis and passed away on December 7, 1981.

The Alameda County Coroner's Office confirmed the cause of death and later tests at the University of California San Francisco Medical Center's Pathology Department showed that Johney had massive quantities of asbestos fibers in his lungs. In March 1982, Randy's mother Juanita came to see me and the family retained us to represent them in a lawsuit against Fibreboard Corporation and the suppliers of asbestos fibers to its factory. In September 1982, we filed suit on behalf of Johney's family – his mother, his sisters, and Randy. We were able to settle that case, but it was several decades ago.

I can't explain exactly how or why I remembered so much about Johney's case, but when I heard Randy's voice on the phone that day, and heard him ask "Do you remember me?", I immediately said, "Of course I do. How are you?" His answer shocked me. "I was just diagnosed with mesothelioma and I was hoping you could help me," he said. And that's how I became involved in the story you are reading about in this book.

In fact, much of Randy's asbestos exposure came when he was a child and young man living in his parents' home, which was contaminated by the asbestos fibers Johney brought home in his hair and on his clothes without having any idea of the dangers they presented to his family. Johney first worked with asbestos starting in 1947 and the house was well contaminated by the time Randy was born in 1955, and it stayed that way until he grew up and left the family home.

While it may sound like an unusual story, in fact, more and more often we are seeing cases of people who were exposed through family members who brought asbestos home from their workplace without knowing the hazards. Sadly, for the second time, I had the privilege to represent the Clemmons family and help them obtain justice for the wrong done to them.

Throughout, Randy went out of his way to make sure my staff and I weren't too upset by his illness. He fought his mesothelioma with all he had, while he continued to live his life with uncommon dignity and grace. We miss him.

How to Choose an Asbestos Attorney: What You Need to Know

If you are suffering from malignant mesothelioma or another type of asbestos-related disease, you are the victim of a wrongdoer. Someone or several someones in a decision-making role chose to expose you and your family to materials containing asbestos fibers even though it has been well-established since the 1920s that prolonged exposure to asbestos fibers can cause fatal illness. These wrongdoers and others like them may be continuing to expose unsuspecting people to asbestos because it serves their business interests to do so. We all have a duty and responsibility to try to stop them and bring them to trial for their wrongdoing so that they pay for the harm they have done to you. You will also be helping to prevent further lawlessness and loss of life. To do so in a way that is meaningful to you and your family and that may help others in a similar situation, you must make a careful decision about which attorney to choose.

Why Choosing an Asbestos Attorney is the Most Important Financial Decision You'll Ever Make

Selecting an attorney to represent you and your family in an asbestos case is the most important financial decision you will ever make.

It is a more important decision than even buying a home. Your home could potentially yield you a couple of hundred thousand dollars in return on investment if property values skyrocket in your neighborhood. But an asbestos case properly handled by a top quality law firm that specializes in asbestos cases can be worth millions to you and your family.

Money cannot replace a person. But money can prevent additional unnecessary suffering on the part of the family by paying the bills. It also helps give you and your family a sense of justice. A great harm was done to you and a good asbestos attorney can make sure that those responsible for this wrongdoing are held accountable, and that the family's financial security is guaranteed.

Your medical care expenses and the loss of earnings as the family breadwinner can be compensated with substantial settlements if you choose your attorney carefully. But what's more, you could potentially – as many of my firm's clients choose to do – set aside a portion of the money you receive for mesothelioma medical research, and we will be honored to contribute to that effort.

You could support a charitable trust to help fund medical research seeking to find a cure and better treatment for mesothelioma. You could help create a future where possibly no one will suffer from the debilitating effects and losses of this disease. This would be money that would never go towards this important cause unless someone like you puts it there. And this would only be possible if you work with attorneys who are experienced and are willing to fight for you every inch of the way, not just take the easy way out and settle for a minimal amount.

Again, this is the most crucial financial decision you will ever make in your life. Getting it wrong could harm your chance of providing your family with financial security for after you're gone.

Starting the Search for an Asbestos Attorney

Mesothelioma lawyers practice in a highly specialized area of the law, representing the victims of asbestos exposure and their families. There are approximately 2,500 new cases of mesothelioma diagnosed each year in the United States. The top attorneys who know the intricacies of asbestos litigation and have the experience to successfully take a case through the court system are in a league of their own and practice only in this area of the law and no other.

If you have been told that you are suffering from mesothelioma, usually as the result of working with asbestos or living with someone who worked with asbestos, you have a very strong chance of receiving a very large sum of money in damages from the companies that manufactured or installed the asbestos components you handled and from bankruptcy trust funds set up to compensate asbestos victims of some of those companies.

But mesothelioma cases are often very complicated because it may take 10 to 40 years after the asbestos exposure for mesothelioma to show symptoms. Having an experienced attorney working on your behalf -one with a record of success in mesothelioma cases and who is well-versed in asbestos law – is key to winning your case.

Finding the best mesothelioma lawyer for your situation can require some time and effort. If you are struggling with mesothelioma and not feeling up to it, please enlist the help of a family member or friend to do the research for you on a lawyer's qualifications and track record. It is important and well worth the effort.

Why You Need an Attorney Who Specializes Only in Asbestos Cases

Your family doctor may be the greatest guy in the world. But would you want him performing open heart surgery on you? Probably not, right? You would want to be in the hands of a competent experienced specialist, in this example, a heart surgeon, trained to be an expert in this specific field of medicine.

Likewise, if you need to bring an asbestos lawsuit to court, you need an attorney who is an expert in this specific area of law. Take my firm for example. We are good at what we do because that is all we do. We do not handle other types of personal injury cases. We only handle asbestos cases and have done so for almost 40 years. If you come to me tomorrow with a medical malpractice case, I will tell you who is the best attorney I think you should go to but I will not take the case. It wouldn't be fair to you.

Let's put it another way. If you go out to eat at a diner or café, the menu usually offers a little bit of everything. There'll be steak, some kind of fish, a pasta dish and a maybe a quiche of the day. These will all fill you up and they will be okay, but they won't be the best. If you want a really good steak, you go to a steakhouse. If you're craving pasta, you go to an Italian restaurant. And for the best fish, you go to a seafood place not a diner. For fantastic French food, you'd go to a French restaurant.

Not everyone can do everything well. That's just reality. Anyone who says he or she handles everything can't be the best at anything. With luck, they'll be okay. But just okay is not good enough for an asbestos case involving suffering and loss of human life.

If you have a trusted family attorney who has helped you with your will or through a divorce, he or she may be a good source to start with to help you find a reliable asbestos attorney. But this would not be someone you should expect to take on your case.

Why You Should Look Beyond Your Community For the Best Asbestos Attorney

Believe it or not, it doesn't really matter where an attorney is geographically located. When it comes to choosing an attorney for an asbestos case, closer is not always better. Working with a highly regarded and experienced mesothelioma attorney is more valuable than having one who is close by. That is truer than ever today, with the expanded capabilities of internet and cell phone communications. An experienced mesothelioma attorney understands that you are not feeling well due to your asbestos-caused illness. They will not expect you to travel to them. They will travel to you. A top-quality asbestos attorney will take the time to come and meet with you no matter where you live. For example, wherever you live in the U.S., you can call us and we will come and help you. It's what we do.

Why is this important? The value of your case and the amount of compensation you receive can vary greatly not only depending on the qualifications of your attorney but also on the city in which the attorney files your case. Juries tend to award more and therefore settlements are higher in big cities with booming economies and high costs of living, like the San Francisco Bay Area, where I practice.

And, often we have several choices. For example, if you were exposed to asbestos while you were in the U.S. Navy stationed in the San Francisco Bay Area, or if the company responsible for your asbestos exposure has its headquarters in the San Francisco Bay Area, we can file the case here, even if you have lived in Iowa ever since. The value of your case would be much higher if it is tried here, with our higher costs of living, than it would be in your home town.

I can understand that someone with mesothelioma in a small town might feel more comfortable just going down to the local courthouse to initiate a lawsuit instead of getting on a plane to do so in some other place. But you likely will never need to travel. We come to you for deposition testimony and trial preparation. Only if your case actually goes to trial (a small percentage of cases do so) might you need to even consider travel.

Analyzing your situation and figuring out the best place to bring an asbestos case takes someone who knows what they're doing. The situation calls for an expert attorney who has the experience and wisdom to know where to bring an individual's asbestos case in order to obtain the best possible outcome.

Please be aware that there are attorneys out there who simply want to make their money the easiest and quickest way possible. They are not looking out for you and your family. They would rather do a mediocre job on a large number of cases than do a really spectacular job on your case. They will file a case wherever it is most convenient, not where it is most likely to yield the highest award amount. For those of you with a really strong case with the potential for a very large award, an attorney like this is not your best option. So put away your local yellow pages and look for the best asbestos attorneys in the entire United States, not just in your town or county. It will be well worth it.

Internet Searches for an Asbestos Attorney - Beware

Have you ever been on vacation and stopped at a touristy shopping area? Where every merchant is frantically trying to get you to come into their store? That's because if they don't get you to come in, they have no chance of selling you something. It's the same on the internet with asbestos attorneys.

The internet ads that flood your computer if you type in "asbestos attorney" or "mesothelioma attorney," will yield a mixed bag of results. Along with a handful of websites for the relatively small number of attorneys in the U.S. who excel in mesothelioma cases, there will be many sites for "attorneys" who really are case brokers all too eager to profit at the expense of someone who is suffering from an illness and does not know how to find a good attorney for his case. They may have a law license but don't really have litigation skills or staff- they will sell your case to a "real lawyer" for a fee.

Also be aware that a website that appears to be a mesothelioma information website could be just a front for a hungry mesothelioma "lawyer". The website may even state that it is run by a nonprofit and have a "dot org" – nonprofit organizations' website names end in .org instead of .com - attached to its name. Any disclosure that it is really a commercial website created to catch new customers for a law firm is only evident in tiny print; probably not even on the website's main page. The site might be loaded with goodies for you just like the witch's gingerbread house that enticed Hansel and Gretel. Only here the goodies the site may claim to offer include patient advocates, patients' stories and special assistance to help veterans, not candy.

Often these phony websites provide a live chat option or a live phone call option, again with the appearance of being a neutral information resource for those concerned about asbestos disease. In truth, they are nothing but a marketing tool used by "lawyers" to capture people's interest and keep them from looking elsewhere on the web for legitimate lawyers.

If you go to my firm's website - www.kazanlaw.com - you can read about our 20 lawyers who work on asbestos cases and about our decades of experience. I'm on the site and so are all my associates. With these phony websites, you don't know who you're really dealing with or what you could be getting yourself into. The people running the site may not be real lawyers. They may just be salespeople who will sell your case to someone for 50% of the final fee the attorney may charge you.

Lawyers and brokers who use fake dot org websites hide who they are. They may call their sites mesothelioma center or mesothelioma assistance center or something like that to keep you from going elsewhere. As long as you are on their site, they've got a shot at getting your business just like the tourist trap shopkeeper.

Our firm also sponsors a nonprofit mesothelioma informational website - www.mesotheliomacircle.org. But its home page has a full disclosure that Kazan Law sponsors the site, and even features my photo. We are not hiding anything or pretending to be something we are not. We are proud of who we are and the work we do on behalf of mesothelioma victims and their families.

I believe that a lawyer should not hide what he or she is doing. If a client/attorney relationship starts out in a lie why would you expect it to get any better?

Carefully read through all the legal information a lawyer provides on their website. Lawyers who provide good thorough information are more likely to be legitimate asbestos attorneys who will be a good fit for your needs. But distrust lawyers who say little more than "I can get you millions right away -- trust me." Take it from me, don't.

10 Quick Tips for Selecting an Asbestos Attorney

When you begin your search, keep in mind that a good asbestos attorney:

1. Knows a lot about mesothelioma and other asbestos-related diseases
2. Has ample experience in filing asbestos legal claims
3. Will be able to tell you whether you have a good case to bring forward
4. Will travel to you
5. Presents themselves openly and honestly on their website
6. Will charge you on a contingency basis
7. Provides you with copies of important documents
8. Does not work through a broker
9. Does not appear in late night TV ads
10. Makes no unrealistic promises

General Guidelines for Choosing an Asbestos Attorney

Coping with mesothelioma is exhausting and overwhelming. It is heroic when you are not feeling well to try to right the wrong done to you. But it is important once you start, to make sure that in the attempt to correct one injustice, you don't create another injustice by working with an inadequate attorney who will not do right by you and your family.

An attorney who specializes in mesothelioma not only is familiar with the disease but also with the legal history of all major asbestos-related cases, and how to fully assess a potential mesothelioma lawsuit. Good mesothelioma attorneys are familiar with not only the important legal decisions; they also stay up to date on asbestos-related cases all over the United States and the world. We use this knowledge to give you a preliminary opinion about your case and later to present the strongest possible case for you, if you engage us to file a claim on your behalf.

The asbestos attorney you choose should be someone whose reputation and experience inspires you with confidence. But it should also be someone with whom you feel comfortable and with whom you will be able to easily talk to about your situation.

Here are some additional guidelines that can help you with this important decision.

Make sure the attorney's fees are on a contingency basis

A contingency fee arrangement is when your lawyer gets a percentage of the compensation award you receive from the resolution of your asbestos lawsuit. If you wind up not receiving any compensation for the lawsuit then your lawyer collects no fees. But you may owe charges for court fees, copying, and hiring expert witnesses. (More about contingency fees below)

Check an attorney's references

A good mesothelioma attorney should be able to provide you with a list of references of several previous clients to contact. Although you will only be given the contact information for very pleased clients, it will still be informative to talk to them about their experiences working with a mesothelioma attorney you are considering hiring for your case.

Don't be Misled by Late Night TV Ads and Fast Talk

TV ads can be appealing. That's why they're there. TV ads for asbestos attorneys are no exception. Because mesothelioma cases can be so profitable, many lawyers spend lots of money on TV ads. These ads may make you want to pick up the phone and call that toll-free number right away. You might even talk to someone who seems knowledgeable and charming. You might say later on down the road, "But he seemed like such a nice guy." Yes, that's why he's on TV. Don't get me wrong. You need to feel comfortable with your asbestos attorney and able to confide in them. But trust me, anyone who comes on strong like they're your new best friend, isn't.

Steer Clear of an Asbestos Case Broker

If you find yourself in the clutches of someone who is more broker than attorney, be skeptical. Especially if they claim that they are going to find you the best asbestos attorney to work for you. Who is this person you're talking to? What's in it for them? Why are they talking to you if they are not the one who is going to be handling your case and doing the work?

A broker will try to peddle your case to the highest bidder. This is not good for you because an attorney who uses a broker may be motivated by how much money they will get to keep from your case. If the broker charges 40 to 50 percent of the attorney's fee, most attorneys would turn that down. The broker will go further down to the bottom of the attorney barrel to find one desperate enough for work to accept the broker's deal. They may not be very good or very experienced and they might not work very hard for you. Instead of climbing to the top of the mountain to get you the best possible outcome, they will take the easy way out and settle so they can go on to the next case. They do quantity not quality work.

Don't go through a broker. They will just turn your case over to any attorney who will pay their finder's fee. They do not have your best interests at heart.

Interview a prospective asbestos attorney

Be sure to interview any attorney you are considering hiring for an asbestos case. If you are not feeling well enough, ask a family member or friend to do this. Request a case evaluation and a personal interview with the attorney at a large firm who would be handling your case. Here are some questions to ask:

12 Questions to Ask a Prospective Asbestos Attorney

1. Who is going to do the work?
2. How will you be paid for your time on my case?

3. What expenses will I be responsible for?
4. Who would I call or email if I have questions?
5. Are you going to do it yourself or are you going to send it to someone else to do?
6. Is your firm going to handle the case all by itself?
7. Who will actually file the lawsuit?
8. Where will the lawsuit be filed?
9. Who is going to work on my case?
10. Who is going to go to court for me?
11. How many years has your law firm been in business?
12. How many asbestos cases have you handled?

Why You Should Only Hire an Attorney Who Will Work on a Contingency Fee

Contingency Fees

The best professional asbestos attorneys in the country will work for you on a contingency basis. What does that mean? That means we are only paid after a judgment has been won or settlements reached in your case. For example, if you retained Kazan Law as your attorneys, you do not pay us up front and you would never get bills from us. We do not charge by the hour. Instead, a portion of the money awarded to you will go to our office and the rest will go to you.

It also means that if you decide to go to trial and the jury decides against you, you will get nothing and will owe us nothing. If we take your case, we take the risk of not being paid.

What is a contingency fee?

253

Most plaintiffs' attorneys in civil cases operate on a contingency fee basis, with some charging up to one-half the recovery; we charge less. Here's how it works with us: say the contingency fee is one-third. Then, for each $1,000 in settlements you get $666.67 (two-thirds) and the attorneys who represent you get $333.33 (one-third.)

Many attorneys take their percentage first and then subtract the costs of the lawsuit out of the client's share. (The "costs" are for things like court filing fees, experts' fees and expenses, medical-legal expenses, court reporters, etc.)

And here's another way our clients benefit. Kazan Law subtracts the costs first – before the money is divided – so that we share the costs with the client. Our clients therefore get a larger proportion of the money awarded.

How do contingency fees work?

For example, if there are $1,000 in settlements and $100 in costs, Kazan Law subtracts the $100 costs from the $1,000, and then we take our contingency fee out of the remaining $900. So you would get $600 and our fee would be $300. However many other attorneys make you pay all the costs. The lawyer takes one-third of the total or $333.33. Your share is $667.67, but out of that, the lawyer takes the $100 for costs, so you get only $567.67 and the lawyer gets $433.33. Which do you like better?

In this example the difference may seem small, but in many of our cases the difference could amount to a hundred thousand dollars or more for you.

How to Get Ready to Talk to an Asbestos Attorney

Before you start the process of researching and choosing an asbestos attorney to handle your case, there are a few things you can do to help kickstart the process. Remember the right attorney will fight for you to receive all the compensation you are due. But even the most experienced asbestos attorney can't do that without some basic information from you about your individual situation. So take a little time to put your information in order so you can be specific when you discuss your case with a prospective attorney. This includes information about:

Your Medical Situation

You will need to provide concrete evidence that you are suffering from mesothelioma so be prepared to provide the:

Date and place of your diagnosis

Name and phone number for the physician who diagnosed you

List of specific treatments and medications prescribed for you and how much you have had to pay out-of-pocket for these.

Your Job History

Your attorney also needs to prove that you developed mesothelioma because you or someone in your family was exposed to asbestos at work and who was responsible. Be prepared to provide:

255

The name of the company you worked for. If the company has been sold to another company, try to find out that name, too.

The dates you worked for the company – when you started and when you stopped. Try to find and make copies of tax returns or W2 forms that support those dates.

The names of products and materials you handled as part of your job

Your job title and specific job duties and job site locations

Conclusion

When mesothelioma symptoms have emerged and a diagnosis is received, that usually means that a case is advanced and time is of the essence. Especially when it comes to presenting a legal case, because even the best-handled legal case can take time. But in addition to legal expertise in mesothelioma and asbestos, we mesothelioma attorneys know a great deal about the disease itself. We understand the challenges that you and your family face following diagnosis with an asbestos-related illness. We also are sensitive to your need to focus on your treatment and time with loved ones. At the same time, we also know that it is important for all involved to file your claim and gather evidence as soon as possible. So I encourage you to proceed into the legal arena with caution and diligence but to proceed.

Asbestos law is a narrow practice area focusing exclusively on asbestos-related disease, typically caused by occupational exposure or military service. The laws and rules regarding winning a lawsuit are complicated. Only expert mesothelioma attorneys have the experience and knowledge necessary to handle your case and secure the justice and compensation you deserve. You and your family are entitled to nothing less than the best. Use this information to make sure you get it. And remember, God is with you.

About Steven Kazan

Steven Kazan is the founding, senior and managing principal of the law firm Kazan, McClain, Satterly, Lyons, Greenwood & Oberman. Steven has played a significant role in asbestos litigation for nearly four decades. Mr. Kazan filed his first case on behalf of an asbestos victim in 1974 and since then has represented thousands of injured workers and their family members in court cases. He has dedicated the majority of his practice to representing workers suffering from mesothelioma in third party asbestos lawsuits (against manufacturers, contractors, distributors, and premises owners). In addition, he has also represented victims of asbestos lung cancer as well as seriously disabling asbestosis.

Steven has also been nominated by the U.S. Trustee and appointed by the U.S. Bankruptcy Court to serve as a member or as counsel to victim members on almost all asbestos bankruptcy reorganizations, including Amatex, Carey Canada, Celotex, H.K. Porter, Babcock & Wilcox, Armstrong World Industries (AWI), W.R. Grace, NARCO, Federal-Mogul, Kaiser

Aluminum, Global Technologies (GIT), ACandS, ARTRA, Owens Corning, Fibreboard, Plibrico, T&N, U.S. Gypsum, Combustion Engineering, the Muralo Company, Congoleum, Flintkote Company, Special Electric, ABB Lummus Global, T H Agriculture & Nutrition, Leslie Controls, Garlock, and General Motors. In almost all cases where the bankruptcy reorganization is approved, He has been approved by the Federal Court to serve as a member of The Trustees' Advisory Committee to work with The Trust on behalf of asbestos victims.

Throughout his career, Mr. Kazan has been a lecturer, speaker, moderator, program chairman and participant at various legal, medical, and insurance seminars and conferences throughout the world focusing on asbestos, toxic torts, and mass torts. He has lobbied and testified in Congress on behalf of asbestos victims and before the Senate and House Judiciary Committees on asbestos litigation and legislation.

Prior to starting the firm in Oakland in 1974, Mr. Kazan was an Assistant to the General Counsel of the Interstate Commerce Commission in Washington, D.C. (1967-1969); an Assistant United States Attorney for the Northern District of California (1969-1971); and an associate at Werchick & Werchick, a plaintiffs' medical malpractice specialty law office in San Francisco (1971-1974.)He graduated from Harvard Law School in 1966 after earning his undergraduate degree from Brandeis University in 1963.

Chapter 24: Resources

Here are the resources we used during Randy's illness. Maybe they could be a comfort to you in this tumultuous time:

Alta Bates Comprehensive Cancer Center

(Dr. David Pfister)Retired
2001 Dwight Way
Berkeley, CA 94704
(510) 204-4214

UCSF Pain Management Center
Dr. George Pasvankas
2255 Post Street
San Francisco, CA 94143
(415) 885-7246
www.ucsfhealth.org

UCSF Comprehensive Cancer Center
Dr. Thierry Jahan (Mesothelioma Specialist)
1600 Divisadero Street, 4th Floor
San Francisco, CA 94115
(415) 353-9888

UCSF Thoracic Surgery Oncology
David M Jablons & Dr. Jasleen Kukreja
1600 Divisadero Street, 4th Floor
San Francisco, CA 94115
(510) 885-3882

Dr. Carol Jessop (Pain Management)

5349 College Ave
Oakland, CA 94618
(510) 547-5111

Steven Kazan (Mesothelioma Lawyer)
Kazan Law
Jack London Market
55 Harrison St., Suite 400
Oakland, CA 94607
1-877-995-6372
www.kazanlaw.com

Made in the USA
San Bernardino, CA
20 January 2014